THE SECRETS OF A FANTASTIC MARRIAGE

BY GREG VIOLI

DER ÜBERWINDER
VERLAG

The Secrets of a Fantastic Marriage

3rd Edition published 2015 by der ÜBERWINDER VERLAG.
Astrid-Lindgren, 32107 Bad Salzuflen, Germany
Design: Jemima Gassmann
Therismos Drukarnia, Wroclaw, Poland.

ACKNOWLEDGMENTS

The author would like to give the greatest appreciation to a God that he has discovered as his Father. It was a wonderful day when he discovered that God, his Father loved him. It was a more wonderful day when he learned that this incredible God not only loved him, but he also liked him and even enjoyed being with him. What a joy to realize that the one who made the universe desires to have an intimate relationship where one can unburden his heart and show his deep inner feelings. Secondly, the author wishes to express his gratitude to his precious wife, Marie. She has spent many hours typing the manuscript and many years loving her husband, especially in the midst of great trials. Lastly, appreciation and love goes out to his family. People that have cried with him, prayed with him, and stood with him even when it seemed he was all alone. Thank you for your patience, love, and support.

TABLE OF CONTENTS

FOREWORD

This small little book is being written because of the urgency of the hour in which we live. My wife and I travel around nations and all throughout the USA. We are coming face to face with a major crisis. This major crisis that I refer to is the pitiable condition of marriages. There is a deep, hidden sense of discouragement, hopelessness, or a satisfaction with a marriage that is far below God's purpose in many lives. The testimonies of God-saturated and joy-filled relationships in marriages are very few. God is primarily a father, and his entire nature is permeated with the revelation of fatherhood. Therefore, it is a deep longing in his holy heart to reveal to the world the true meaning of family.

First and foremost, it must be recognized that God originated, designed, and purposed the marital relationship between a man and woman with the intention that there would be great blessings for each partner. A little personal background would be helpful to the reader of this book. I grew up in a large, religious family with four sisters and three brothers, of which I was the second youngest child. In the nineteen years I lived at home, most of my memories are comprised of great tension, fear, screaming, a lot of joking, and mocking with no memory of kind words spoken.

Every one of the eight children has memories of being told about our adulterous father and his family's hatred towards our mother. At times, my mother would take me to church for the 5:30am service. I remember going to church and hearing about how we should live our life. Unfortunately, what I was witnessing at home was so much different from what I was hearing at church. I have many memories of my mother screaming in the middle of the night, as I would be suddenly awakened out of sleep. In no way do I intend to criticize or blame my family or parents for my upbringing. Actually, I believe that we all did the best that we knew how to do. My mother was raised by a mother that screamed and yelled a lot, and when she found out that our grandfather was killed in the coalmines of Pennsylvania, she was glad.

So many people, like myself, carry the ripple effects of abuse and hatred. A stone is thrown into the pond and it goes down to the bottom, but the effects of it hitting the water remains in the form of ripples. When someone is wounded, the effects of that wound are often carried for a long time. If any form of hatred is not cleansed out of us by the blood of Jesus, then it must remain in us. My wife was raised by an alcoholic father and a mother who had many cares and worries that are common with the dysfunctional history of alcoholism in a family. Once again, I want to state that my only purpose in sharing this negative history of our upbringing is that others might benefit and find the tremendous healing and restoration like we have found. Both of our families tried, but the result of their efforts was more wounded dysfunctional behavior.

Marie and I were put together by God with our unhealed issues to form our own family in1980. For the last thirty-four years, both Marie and I would have to declare that our married life and our family environment has basically been heaven on earth. Jesus Christ said, *"The kingdom of heaven is within you"* (Luke 17:21b).

What you are about to read are the truths and secrets that the Lord has been teaching us over the last thirty years. "Go ye therefore and teach all nations, baptizing them in the name of the Father and of the Son and of the Holy Ghost; teaching them to observe all things whatsoever I have commanded you: and, lo, I am with you always, even until the end of the world. Amen" (Matthew 28:19–20).

One final comment is that we were advised by others of certain things we needed to make our marriage work: 1) money and a bank account—we didn't have any; 2) a good job that had a future with a good salary—we didn't have one; 3) time to get to really know each other (communicative skills)—we didn't have much time to know each other. Mostly everything we were told by others that we needed, we did not have. But by the mercy of God, we did discover the main ingredients for a fantastic marriage!

In the love of Jesus,
Greg Violi

INTRODUCTION

This book is intended to make good marriages fantastic, bad marriages fantastic, and hopeless marriages fantastic; and is intended to lay a foundation of how engaged couples can experience a fantastic marriage. It is time for the world to behold marriage as God always intended it to be. The marriage relationship was meant to show all creation how God's very own heart of love draws and woos his bride unto himself and then how the bride responds to this extravagant, pure love with joyful, lowly submission.

Typical remarks made by individuals going through a bad marriage are:

"I just don't love him any more."
"I never should have married her."
"There's no hope, it's hopeless."
"This can never work."
"I married the wrong person."
"I'll show him."
"We've tried counseling."
"He never changes."
"I can never forgive her."

"It's too late."
"I don't feel anything."
"It would be better for everyone if we separate."

All of the above are spoken, but there are far more things that are not spoken but are meditated on the inside. These things cause even more problems than the things that are spoken. God's love does not think evil.

Here are some things that struggling couples meditate on:
"I'll get even."
"I wish he felt the pain that he has made me feel."
"I'll show her."
"Who does he think he is?"
"Why did she do that?"
"He'll get what he deserves."
"I wish she were dead."
"I hate him."
"It would be so much better without her."

All of these thoughts come with the intention of stealing, killing, and destroying what God is trying to orchestrate. The Holy Spirit is looking for helpless, hopeless situations to show his almighty power through, and then the people involved and the onlookers will all acknowledge that "only God could have done it." He will get all the credit and glory for totally healing and transforming their marriage. My wife and I have seen so many marriages totally healed that we are certain, through God's grace, your marriage and life will never be the same after reading this book.

Throughout this book, the cross will be viewed as the very power of God for salvation to all who believe. Salvation is an all-inclusive word, and it comprehends being saved from wrath, deliverance, healing, wholeness, freed, being made whole, etc. When a person goes to the cross, he is taking all of the power of evil that has come against his life and bringing it to be destroyed through the power of the blood of Jesus Christ. When someone goes to the cross with all their pain, sin, and the sins of others, then the very evil that was meant to destroy them is now destroyed by the power of God's love at Calvary.

Throughout this book, I teach how to apply the cross of Jesus Christ to meet every need and to destroy all the evils that one has or will encounter in this world. When Jesus died on the cross, he was destroying all power of the evil one. See 1 John 3:8 and Hebrews 2:14.

By his stripes (the severe beatings), we are healed. Therefore, when a person takes all their sin, sickness, oppression, fears, etc. to the cross where Jesus was severely beaten, all of the pain is now absorbed by the Lord, and he releases healing in the place of their sores. *"But he was wounded for our transgressions, he was bruised for our iniquities: the chastisement of our peace was upon him; and with his stripes we are healed"* (Isaiah 53:5).

For example, when a woman chooses to carry the pain of what someone did to her, then she will continue to experience the memories and sorrows and the anger associated with that specific pain. But when she goes to the cross and pronounces forgiveness for the offender, then she herself will experience the healing that mercy and love brings.

The cross is more than a historical event that occurred about two thousand years ago. The cross represents a supernatural act of divine love and power, and anyone who believes and takes their sins and the sins of others to the cross will then experience its power. Love will always overcome, and God will always overcome evil. The power of the cross will be revealed throughout this entire book.

15 SIGNS OF A FANTASTIC MARRIAGE

1. A lifestyle filled with peace no matter what the circumstances.
2. Joy in the midst of suffering, a deep joy that comes from the pleasure of pleasing God in one's life.
3. Living above problems. You have problems, but they do not have you!
4. A feeling of kindness, love and appreciation that gets stronger and stronger as time goes on. This feeling is strong during the day, but at night it is the strongest. You feel deep love and appreciation as you just hold your spouse in your arms.
5. A real passionate desire to be intimate with the one that God has given you. The two shall be one flesh.
6. Many kisses and "I love yous" during the week.
7. Absolutely no desire to embarrass or to put down your beloved in the presence of family, friends or strangers.
8. A home environment that is full of the presence of Jesus. This is due mainly to the fact Jesus loves to dwell where there is love.
9. Times of sexual intimacy that are very enjoyable without hard feelings before, during or after sex.

10. The blessings of God increase because He has promised to give us all things if we put his kingdom and righteousness first.
11. Life becomes enjoyable because He gives us all things to enjoy. This includes enjoying raising children, cleaning the home, working at the job and maturing through life. Life is not seen as a burden, stress and tension are replaced with love.
12. The children and grandchildren are greatly blessed through the lives of the parents. These are real blessings from God's perspective, not from man's perspective.
13. The world beholds God in the midst of this couple. The heart of Jesus can be seen as the husband loves his wife and the wife submits to her husband.
14. The heart attitude of worship starts to saturate the very atmosphere of the home and the children or grand -children are experiencing the pleasure of God's heart. The Lord's joy is released because he is pleased with the heart attitudes of the father and mother.
15. Since whatever we sow, we shall reap, the very attitude of giving starts to invade other members of the family. As the couple releases the heart of giving, it will fill the hearts of others within the family. Their whole attitude becomes one of being a blessing, therefore they receive great blessing. Some forms of blessings are:
    a) to find purpose and destiny in one´s life.
    b) to experience deep joy and peace. (peace is the absence of strife and tension)
    c) to have your needs met emotionally, physically, spiritually and mentally.

These are fifteen signs that a couple is living in the reality of a fantastic marriage.

CHAPTER ONE

THE DIVINE PURPOSE FOR MARRIAGE

To begin this book, I want to give my own meaning of the word fantastic. Fantastic means totally beyond the normal experience and extravagantly wonderful to behold and witness.

"The Lord God said, 'It is not good that the man should be alone; I will make him an help meet for him'" (Genesis 2:18). God is declaring specific truths in this simple statement. The first truth is that it is God's idea that man should not be alone. Next, man should find fulfillment by the addition of a necessary part, which is the woman. Since woman was taken out of man, he will always feel emptiness without her. It is only when a man is given a special gift by God to be alone can he sustain and be fulfilled by himself, but this is not the original plan of God. God is truth, and when he declares something, he means it! Loneliness is a curse on many a life. Oftentimes, when a person is seen alone in a crowd, it is due to one of three things: 1) unhealed inner issues of rejection, self-hatred, and abuse, or 2) the fruit of a life where hatred has been its environment 3) a self centered life.

UNHEALED INNER ISSUES

Abusive relationships in childhood will leave devastating effects on a person, and that person will feel nobody wants them or they do not deserve to be alive or they do not fit in the crowd.

Most of the time, these feelings come out of self-hatred, rejection, fear, and bitterness. When there is (on the inside) defilement within the soul of a person, nothing looks pure on the outside. See Titus 1:15.

One example of this sort of unhealed issue is a woman getting ready for her wedding but she often feels totally inadequate, inferior, jealous, and unloved by her fiancé. The truth is that her fiancé thinks she is beautiful, special and he's excited about becoming her husband. The real reason she is tormented is because her father abandoned her and relatives physically and emotionally abused her, rejected her, and spoke negative about her! Now her emotions and memories are being triggered whenever she has an experience or feeling that reminds her of her past abusive treatment from others. She must now take her memories with the offenses of others to the cross and allow the mercy and love of Jesus to wash away the pain of past hurts and sins.

Lastly, she must walk in faith and refuse to receive any thoughts that the enemy will give her regarding her past negative experiences and love others and herself no matter how she feels. She must choose to love herself because she is greatly loved by God. Now, she will experience the truth that by his stripes she is healed.

THE FRUIT OF A LIFE WHERE HATRED HAS BEEN ITS ENVIRONMENT

God pronounced a curse on Cain after he killed his brother Abel (see Genesis 4:10–12). It is written that whoever rewards evil for good, evil shall not depart from his house (see Proverbs 17:13). When a child grows up within an environment of hate, he shall reap the fruit of hatred and loneliness. Cain's hate was from the wicked one (see 1 John 3:12a). Whatever a man sows, he shall reap (see Galatians 6:7b). If a family sows hatred within their home environment; then the children will reap the effects of that hatred in their lives. The fruit of Cain's hatred was that he was to live his life as a wanderer and a vagabond on the earth.

When someone is bearing the fruit of hatred, they might feel like they never fit in with any group of people. The truth might be that they are very important and others look up to them, but the fruit of living in an atmosphere of hatred is the feeling of isolation. After Cain killed Abel, he went on to have a descendant, Lamech, who killed two people. The fruit of Cain's hatred was now multiplying in Cain's descendants. Many times people are carrying in their personal lives the fruit of what has been sown into them.

All throughout history, it has been proven that the iniquity of fathers has been visited and sown into lives of their sons and daughters (see Exodus 20:5b). A dear sister had been under the effects of her father's ungodly, abusive life. For many years she carried a deep sense of never fitting in or having purpose in her life. When she forgave her father for his hate and abuse, God lifted off of her all the effects of isolation, sadness, and loneliness. *"For he that sows to his flesh shall of the flesh reap corruption; but he that sows to the Spirit shall of the Spirit reap life everlasting."* See Galatians 6:8.

When a person receives the merciful heart of Jesus, they will start to reap life. Whatever a person sows, this shall he also reap. Hatred is of the wicked one and love and mercy is of the Holy One. Doing evil in return for good brings a curse, but doing good in return for evil brings great blessings.

A SELF-CENTERED LIFE

Jesus said unless a corn of wheat falls into the ground and dies, it abides alone (see John 12:24). A person, who has not died to his own selfishness, will spend much time alone. The more pre-occupied we are with ourselves, the more we feel our loneliness. The more preoccupied we are with being a blessing to God and others, the more we feel fulfillment in "just living."

Next, if it is not good for a man to be alone, then it must be bad or evil for a man to be alone. There are many consequences and much good that is relinquished through a man being without a helpmate.

Thirdly, man will find a great delight, satisfaction, and a deep sense of goodness when he accepts God's gift of woman. When a man loves his wife, he is actually loving a part of himself (Ephesians 5:28, 29).

THE JOY OF JUST BEING

In summary, contentment for a person begins with the joy and satisfaction of just being alive. Maybe this is why we are called human beings. The greatest focus should be on being and not on doing. Many times spouses start to feel guilty because they are not doing anything. The accuser will start to make a wife or husband feel guilty because they are not doing something and they are just a mother or father. After Adam and Eve disobeyed God, their true self died, and a false self was formed. The true self finds its fulfillment in just being. "For in him we live, and move and have our being" (see Acts 17:28a). The true self learns to love life and enjoy just being—being with God, being with family, and being with others. The false self is constantly striving to find its fulfillment by having possessions and doing things. A person living in the false self will be driven from within and, therefore, will tend to be a tense person. The true self finds its satisfaction and delight in just living in God, and then out of this sense of fulfillment, this one will find the strength and power to do the "thing at hand." The false self has to do more and have more in order that satisfaction might be experienced. More and more emphasis gets placed on all that one must do, so this individual called to be a helpmate starts to feel guilty and useless, while the emphasis gets placed more and more on doing and the vital importance of being is slowly lost completely.

To understand this more clearly, let's restate it this way: "it is not good for a man to be alone." Therefore, it is good for a man to be with a woman. The first good in the life of a woman is to be with her husband, and the first good in the life of a man is to be with his wife. Our Christianity must begin in our home. The true test of one's Christianity will always be in the home. My life with my family is of utmost importance to God. A man should see the good in being with his wife, and the woman should see the good in just being with her husband.

Now, once this is clearly realized, then one can start to reach out to Judea, Samaria, and even to the ends of the earth. Jesus said but ye shall receive power after that the Holy Ghost is come upon you, and ye shall be witnesses unto me, both in Jerusalem (home), and in all Judea (surrounding areas), and in Samaria (enemies), and unto the uttermost part of the earth.How can my witness be effective and authentic to the uttermost parts of the earth if my witness of Christ is not effective and authentic at home?

GOD'S PARTNER IS PERFECT

Every youth should believe that God has a good and wonderful plan for their life and it includes that they should not be alone. Remember, it was the mouth of God that spoke these words, and man shall live by every word that comes out of the mouth of God (see Deuteronomy 8:3 and Matthew 4:4). *"The thief cometh not, but for to steal, and to kill, and to destroy: I am come that they might have life, and that they might have it more abundantly"* (John 10:10).

Once a single individual trusts in the loving and wise plan of father God for his life, then he should also realize that it is the Lord who has the right person chosen for him. *"O Lord, I know that the way of man is not in himself: it is not in man that walketh to direct his steps"* (Jeremiah 10:23).

Therefore, he needs the counsel and wisdom of God to direct him in the way he should go (see Proverbs 3:5–6). If a person makes their own choice of a lifetime partner without seeking the counsel of almighty God, they could be easily deceived. The more an individual learns to trust in God, the more his decisions will be effective and fruitful.

God loves to place the lonely, solitary ones into beautiful loving families (see Psalm 68:5–6). He is a father, and he loves for families to reveal his divine character to the world.

THE RULER WHO IS ALSO CALLED TO BE A WOOER

What is the main purpose for a couple to be married? It is to reveal the very love of God that draws his bride unto himself and then the joyful, lowly submission of the bride for her husband. God's love draws his people unto himself. See Hosea 11:4a. A husband is to allow the love of God to so fill his heart that he will then draw his beloved unto himself with the cords of love. *"Husbands, love your wives, even as Christ also loved the church, and gave himself for it"* (Ephesians 5:25).

This holy demonstration of love will then cause a response of pure, submissive love from the wife. See Ephesians 5:24. This thorough overflowing of pure love will reveal to others the heart of God, and the beauty of his heart and Father will show the world the extravagant beauty and power of his love. Never is it a demonstration of God's heart when a husband demands submission from his wife. This attitude in a husband will always come from fear, anger, or other evils within his heart that he needs the Lord to cleanse and heal!

Another purpose of marriage is to reproduce a godly seed. Out of love comes a godly seed. The prophet Malachi said that God made the two one so that he might have a godly seed. Therefore, he says, take heed to your spirit that ye do not deal treacherously with the wife of your youth. See Malachi 2:15.

If the invisible part of man (spirit) isn't guarded, then evil will enter, the spouse will be defiled, and the seed will be contaminated. How many Christian spouses have not taken heed to their spirits and cleansed their spirits from everything that defiles it. *"Having therefore these promises, dearly beloved, let us cleanse ourselves from all filthiness of the flesh and spirit, perfecting holiness in the fear of God"* (2 Corinthians 7:1).

There is an eternal principle in the universe, and it is that every seed must bear fruit after its very own kind. See Genesis 11:11–12; Matthew 12:33; Luke 6:44.

Whatsoever we sow, we shall reap. Every seed in thought, word, or deed will be reaped in an abundance of fruit. It is a beautiful, lovely sight to behold the fruit of peace that was sown in the spirits of children by their parents. *"And the fruit of righteousness is sown in peace of them that make peace"* (James 3:18).

One of the most vital tools God gives a person is to take heed to his spirit, and this results in the gift of his very own peace. We are told in Colossians 3:15 to let the peace of Christ rule in your heart. This word for rule means to make the final decision like a referee or umpire. If God withdraws his peace from my heart, then he is notifying me that I need to make an adjustment somewhere in my life. I either opened my spirit to the poison of pride (through unrighteous judging or criticism), or I have made a decision out of my pride. See 1 Peter 5:5. Somewhere in my heart, I received the poison of pride, and therefore, the Lord is resisting me in my pride.

By confessing my wrong, my inner-man is cleansed, and my spirit is purified. If fathers or mothers allow jealousy and strife into their hearts, then there is confusion and every evil thing in their home. See James 3:16. If parents keep their hearts pure and full of love then the fruit of the Spirit will fill their home. This is a lovely sight to behold, and it releases a beautiful atmosphere of peace. Our family has experienced the enjoyment of each other's company, the beautiful sense of God's presence, and the peace of Christ for almost thirty years. By focusing our thoughts on Christ Jesus, our hearts and minds are kept in perfect peace.

The last purpose of marriage is to thoroughly enjoy each other and to multiply righteousness, peace, and joy throughout the whole earth.

THE SECRET OF CHILD BIRTH

I have counseled many couples that were trying to have children but were unsuccessful. I have discovered that if the husband and wife will just enjoy each other and love each other; then their times of sexual intimacy will be filled with joy, excitement, love, and passion. It is within this environment that babies were meant to be born. Out of the union of love will come the fruit of love, which is a new baby. I know couples that could not have children, and after they took out of their hearts every obstacle to love, they were then able to enjoy sex and to love each other and the fruit of that love was a baby. If a couple has fear and they are fearful of not being able to conceive, then this could hinder them from having children and allowing God's perfect love to flow through them. We have counseled several Christian couples who were unsuccessful in bearing children until they simply allowed the river of God's love to flow through them during times of sexual intercourse. God says in his word that perfect love will cast out fear.

God gives us all things to enjoy. In order for this to happen, there has to be a multiplication of people and the reproduction of God's nature through people. Intimate times of physical enjoyment and pure love are meant to be the very environment that a new baby is birthed into. When parents have hard, angry, fearful, or bitter feelings during times of sexual intercourse, these very attitudes will pollute the small little life as he is brought into the world. The unborn child is a spirit with a soul that is beginning to form a physical body, and so it will receive much information from its parents before it ever comes out of the womb.

Lastly, to have children is a glorious blessing and should be a joyful exciting time for parents, family, and loved ones to share. All throughout Scripture, children are considered a blessing and not a burden, and when marriage is fulfilling its God-given purposes, these precious new lives will enrich the world with their very presence and will be a cause of great celebration. I must conclude chapter one by declaring that I do not believe a Christian couple should be satisfied at all with a good marriage. They should expect a fantastic marriage in the power of the Holy Spirit.

CHAPTER TWO

THE MAIN FORCE USED TO DESTROY A MARRIAGE

In this section, the number one, most powerful weapon used by the evil one to destroy a marriage will be exposed. I have personally witnessed hundreds of marriages totally healed and transformed all over the world due to the truth contained in this chapter. There is only one force used by the enemy of our souls on which all the other evils are relying. If this one thing can be destroyed or removed, then all the other evil acts will cease in our society. This one evil attitude of heart is the main force of Satan to advance and maintain his kingdom. The kingdom of darkness would be totally destroyed if this one evil force could be denied.

What is so powerful that it could destroy an entire family and then destroy and work havoc in the next twenty generations to follow and thereby work devastation and ruin in the lives of millions? For a more thorough explanation of the truth contained in this chapter, read the author's books: The Lamb's Heart, The King's Holy Beauty, and Whose Image? The most powerful weapon to destroy a marriage is a heart lifted up in pride. As devastating as pride is in its consequences, it is even more destructive in its ability to deceive and to hide. Pride has an amazing ability to cause people that are being destroyed by it to be totally ignorant of its existence in one's life. This ignorance of pride's existence within an individual is due to the ignorance of what God says about the nature and consequence of pride. Therefore, our first step to expose this deadly virus will be to give some Bible references to God's attitude toward a heart of pride.

THE BIBLICAL DESCRIPTION OF PRIDE

Everyone that is proud in heart is an abomination to the Lord: though hand joins in hand, he shall not be unpunished.

Proverbs 16:5

The Lord will destroy the house of the proud.

Proverbs 15:25a

Pride goeth before destruction, and a haughty spirit before a fall.

Proverbs 16:18

Before destruction the heart of man is haughty, and before honor is humility.

Proverbs 18:12

For the day of the Lord of hosts shall be upon every one that is proud and lofty, and upon every one that is lifted up; and he shall be brought low.

Isaiah 2:12

For he was marvelously helped, till he was strong. But when he was strong, his heart was lifted up to his destruction.

2 Chronicles 26:15c, 16a

But when his heart was lifted up, and his mind hardened in pride, he was deposed from his kingly throne, and they took his glory from him.

Daniel 5:20

And whosoever shall exalt himself shall be abased; and he that shall humble himself shall be exalted.

Matthew 23:12

And immediately the angel of the Lord smote him, because he gave not God the glory.

Acts 12:23a

God resisteth the proud, but giveth grace unto the humble.

James 4:6

These are a few of the hundreds of references in the Word of God about how God feels about pride. God said that he will resist the proud. Everyone that is proud in heart is an abomination to God. God opposes and pronounces judgment on pride. Both Proverbs 6:16, 17, and 8:13 say that God hates pride. Finally, the Lord has made two powerful promises: 1) a day that he will bring down every single person that is lifted up in pride; 2) he will destroy the house of the proud.

Now, if God has promised to destroy the house of the proud, then what hope is there for someone's marriage to be healed? Dear ones, when a person walks in pride, this forces God to become his enemy because the Lord shall always be the enemy of this proud heart, which comes from the evil one! Now, both God and Satan are opposing this person—Satan because he hates all of God's creatures and God because he hates pride! He has to oppose the very thing that he has kicked out of heaven. Therefore, until pride is confronted by the couple, their marriage will not be healed. They must learn to hate these attitudes of pride that are destroying their marriage. What exactly is pride? Pride is when the invisible part inside of a person, called the heart, is lifted up, and in this exalted state it looks down on others, despises them, and places itself on the throne to rule. Pride will cause an individual to be insensitive and unconcerned about the spouse's needs.

MAN-EATING LIONS DO NOT MAKE GOOD PETS

Jesus said that if a person is going to follow him, then this man or woman must do two things: 1) deny self 2) take up his cross. Self can be compared to a man-eating lion. When this ferocious beast is a brand new cub, he is so cute and lovable, and the family plays with him and treats him as their friend. But, in a matter of time, this vicious beast will get larger and more and more of his inner nature will start to emerge and express itself through his personality. There have been quite a few stories over the years about lions and tigers mauling their owners or their owner's family members.

Lions and tigers were destined to live in the world, but if a person treats them as a pet, there will probably come a day when this beast will turn to its true nature and forsake the environment that it is now living in. This is the way that self operates within the life of a person. Self is totally determined to honor itself, exalt itself, feed itself, benefit itself, comfort itself, and for only one main person: itself. This is why Jesus said we must deny self. If a person will not deny self, then eventually the very thing that is not denied starts to control and rule that one's very life. Either I deny self, or self will eventually destroy me.

If a husband and wife do not deny self, God will not give them a fantastic marriage.

So, another way to define pride is selfishness or the self taking first place in my life. Why is this so deadly? The reason it is so deadly is because love does not seek its own. See 1 Corinthians 13:5. There is no selfishness in the heart of love. In the presence of pride, love does not live.

In the presence of love, pride does not live. For example, love is patient and kind. Pride is rude and harsh. Love never holds a grudge. Pride will hold grudges. Love is not puffed up. Pride is always puffed up.

When the nature of pride, which is the nature of Satan, went inside of man in the Garden of Eden, then the nature of God, which is love, had to leave. Love will not stay where pride is allowed to live. There is not one single reference to pride in a good way in the entire Bible, but there are hundreds of Bible verses to share the abomination and evil of pride in the sight of God.

Pride will blind me, deceive me, embitter me, control me, poison me, and will definitely make me insensitive and hard to those I should love. The one thing that seemed to cause Jesus to be angry and deeply grieved was when religious leaders could be insensitive, hard-hearted, and uncaring towards needy broken people. This attitude of pride will cause husbands to judge and condemn their wives, and pride will cause wives to judge and condemn their husbands. If there has been one major secret that my wife Marie and I have discovered to enjoy a fantastic marriage, it is the danger of making judgments, especially on one another. Judgments that I am referring to are the ones that come out of our heart and make us feel hard on the inside toward another person. This hard feeling is almost always a sure sign that an unrighteous judgment has been made. I have probably made an unrighteous judgment on someone.

There are hundreds of couples that we have watched be released from a hard feeling toward their spouse, and after they take the blame for their judgments on each other, then God pours this supernatural divine love into them. In almost every one of our meetings, there are couples that do not sit near each other, but during the service, they get closer and closer to one another. This is due to the fact that their hearts are softening and God is revealing to them how he sees their spouse. Interestingly, God does not see others the way we tend to envision them.

There are many places in the Bible where we are admonished not to judge, lest we be judged.

Judge not, that ye be not judged.

Matthew 7:1

In Ezekiel 7:27b the literal meaning for the verse is *"according to their judgments, will I judge them."*

Who are thou that judgest another man's servant? To his own master he standeth or falleth. Yea, he shall be holden up: for God is able to make him stand.

Romans 14:4

Let us not therefore judge one another any more.

Romans 14:13a

There is one lawgiver, who is able to save and to destroy; who are thou that judges another.

James 4:12

The evil principle behind unrighteous judgments on others is that we are exalting ourselves by making judgments on others. In our self-exaltation, we are declaring that these people, whoever they are, do not deserve mercy. So all unrighteous judgments of others is an inner refusal to give mercy, and Jesus said, "If I don't forgive, then I cannot be forgiven. In Matthew 18:35, Jesus said that our heavenly Father will deliver us to the tormentors if we do not forgive from the heart. I have never known a person with un-forgiveness that was not tormented. The very attitude in the heart of a person that judges another enslaves them and torments them until they forgive and bring the offense of the other to the cross. The cross will now release its power to heal and deliver from evil. By his stripes, we are healed.

YOU ARE NOT EXCUSED

> *Therefore thou art inexcusable, O man, whosoever thou art that judgest: for wherein thou judgest another, thou condemnest thyself; for thou that judgest doest the same things.*
>
> Romans 2:1

This verse brings out the truth that wherever you judge another you condemn yourself. The reason you are condemned is because what you are judging in another, you already are doing in your own flesh nature. There is nothing good in our flesh, and if we have not actually committed an evil, it is not because it is not in us but because God's grace has prevented us from doing it. But, when a person judges another, they are declaring to God that they are not like that other person because of their own goodness and not because of God's grace. All of our judgments on others are declaring to God that we are not like other people because of our own goodness. The truth is that without God's mercy and grace, we could be just as evil as any human being. Our judgments reveal our pride in our own achievements. If a person really thought their achievements were due to the grace of God, then they would not be quick to make judgments on others for their failures. Judgments are often made upon information that is incomplete and partial. We make a judgment based on something we heard or something someone saw, but very often, this is only an incomplete understanding of what really happened.

Now, when we make these judgments on anyone, three things occur:

1) our heart gets hard;
2) we make it necessary for God to remove his grace from that area of our life;
3) now we since we only stand by grace (see 1 Corinthians 15:10), will fall in the same area in which we judged the other.

It is just as wrong for a human being to stand in judgment against an evil as it is wrong to commit an evil. Whenever I stand in judgment against an evil, I am taking God's place as the judge. There is only one judge in the entire universe. See James 4:12. Our opinions are oftentimes judgments that we are making against those "evil people." Justice is very important, but only with the right people at the right time. For example, police officers need to make judgments on criminals, parents need to discipline children school teachers need to make administrative decisions for the good of the entire class, and earthly judges need to make correct verdicts on their subjects. These are all acceptable and necessary, but to judge someone as to being different from myself and not to allow them mercy is to have un-forgiveness in my heart, and this is unacceptable. Instead of judging them, we should feel compassion and ask God for mercy on them.

Anyone that I judge, I now start to see in a different light. Their bad becomes horrible. Their good seems bad. Their innocence becomes guilty, and I can no longer love them or help them. It is impossible to love someone that I have judged in my heart. This is why Jesus Christ could love the whole world. He refused to judge them. The judge will one day deal with the proud rebellious heart of mankind. Judgments are extremely destructive and debilitating, especially in the context of a marriage relationship. I can think of two couples that had their marriage totally healed, and they were experiencing joy, peace, and love in a way that they had not ever felt. After time, the partners in the marriages made judgments and then their love started to become cold toward each other, and it was only a matter of time until their cold love stopped the fire of God's love from burning inside of them. This will always be the fruit of making unrighteous judgments on others.

If a boy judged a woman, such as a mother, aunt, or babysitter, then his judgment will become a root of bitterness waiting to defile many. See Hebrews 12:15. I can remember as I looked into their eyes, beholding the pain, grief, sorrow, and bitterness looking back at me because I had seen these hidden areas of darkness so many times, I knew there were roots of bitterness and judgments inside of both of them. Things like misogyny (hatred of women), sexual abuse as a child, humiliation, defilement, and words that brought death were discovered, repented of, and renounced. Today, they are a loving, happy, Christian couple on their way to a fantastic marriage. By his stripes, we are healed.

A wife will suffer from her husband's past judgments on any female. Likewise, any judgments the wife made on men (father, brothers, uncle, etc.) will now become a root of bitterness, and the main person that will suffer will be her husband. When we take out all of our past and present judgments, then our heart can be tender and good soil for the living Word of God to dwell in. The Lord is looking for the right soil to plant his seed (the incorruptible seed). This seed will also bear fruit after its own kind, and this will be the life and nature of the Lord Jesus Christ.

Someone who is bound by pride will not want to take the blame for any marital problems, and they would rather find excuses than to take the blame. Being right has more significance to a proud person than the success of their marriage.

Pride in the heart of one person will cause this one to be insensitive and hurt their spouse and children. Pride in the spouse and children will cause them to respond in anger and retaliate. If pride is ignored in a family, then it (pride) will continue to cause offenses and wounds in the family. The answer is to start to destroy the power of pride, and it involves eight steps.

1. Confess every sin and judgment to God the Father, and ask for and receive forgiveness.
2. Bring every judgment to the cross, and the cross will break the effects of each judgment.
3. Confess every wrong done to each member in the family. Ask each other forgiveness. Take the blame.
4. Allow Jesus to reveal to you what your own pride has done to others.
5. Stop focusing on what others did to you.
6. Start over today by making the choice to be a vessel for Jesus to love through.
7. Ask Jesus to look through your eyes and to show you what your spouse looks like from his perspective.
8. Ask Jesus to fill your heart with his own compassion.

CHAPTER THREE

FOUR GREAT BLESSINGS THAT A HUSBAND BRINGS INTO THE FAMILY

A man will be as a hiding place from the wind, and a cover from the tempest, as rivers of water in a dry place, as the shadow of a great rock in a weary land.

Isaiah 32:2 (nkjv)

When a man is filled with the Spirit of Jesus, he shall be four major blessings to his wife and children. First, he will be a hiding place from the wind. The wind can blow dust particles into the eye of a person, and these particles can cause great pain and irritation to the individual. A God-possessed man will be a safe place for his wife and children to find security from the irritations and frustrations of life. During windy times, people are seeking a place of safety and security. They need a place to just remain until the wind passes by them. A man through trusting God and being filled with the peace of God will be this place of safety for his wife and children. Next, a man shall be a covering from the tempest of life. The enemy will often try to stir up the waves of adversity within a family. Sometimes, these waves come through the onslaught of negative, critical comments made by others. The enemy will try to use the critical heart of others to condemn and criticize those we love. Sometimes there are financial problems that are overwhelming us like torrents of water in a flood. A man needs to be the covering for his family during these times of conflict and fear.

The husband can be compared to an umbrella on a rainy day. If the umbrella has holes in it, then it will not be a good covering during times of heavy storms. If I have uncleanness, hatred, or resentment in my heart as a husband, then there will be holes in my umbrella. I will have openings through which the enemy will enter to attack my innocent family.

> *Be sober, be watchful, your adversary the devil as a roaring lion walks about seeking whom he is allowed to devour.*
>
> 1 Peter 5:8a

This is mainly referring to Christian families. The devil is already devouring people in the world; they are already under his power. See 1 John 5:19.

It is those dear people who desire to please God that the devil seeks to harass. It is the followers of Christ that he is seeking to devour and he can only touch those whom he has been given permission to touch. Ephesians 4:27 says that we are to give no place to the devil. Pride or selfishness, which always will result in a bad attitude, will give a place for the devil. If there is agreement in my heart with the powers of darkness, then they have a legal right to oppress me. How can two walk together, Amos said, unless they are in agreement? Paul said, what fellowship does light have with darkness? When a husband or father allows evil in his heart by watching pornography, lusting after women, lying, stealing, hating, and yelling at his children instead of disciplining them in love, then he is opening a doorway for the powers of darkness to enter into his family, and he is uncovering his family. In the Scriptures, this is referred to as being naked before our enemies. When the one, God has made, to be leader over his family enters into any form of selfishness or hatred, he is exposing his innocent family to the forces of evil through his own selfishness. Instead of being the covering in the tempest, he is inviting the enemy to come into his family like a flood. It is a great blessing for a father to be this covering over his wife and children in the midst of the tempest.

Third, a man shall be as rivers of water in a dry and thirsty land. A man shall be rivers of refreshment to his wife and children. When they feel tired or ready to give up, dad's presence should bring refreshing rivers into the very atmosphere of the home. The opposite of rivers of water is when a family has to be real quiet in dad's presence, lest he be upset. Selfishness can make the leader of the family only see his own interest and his own needs, and therefore, a husband and father can be very insensitive to the needs of his wife and children.

Rivers of water and not frozen ice cubes. If the man's heart is hard, the family will have to walk around as if they were treading on ice that could crack at any moment. Again, it is a great blessing for a man to be rivers of water in the dry times of daily living.

Fourth, a man shall be as the shade of a great rock in the desert. In other words, when a person is in the desert, there is only one place to find any comfort and shelter and that is in the shade. There is no other place that could possibly give a person any relief in a desert. Everything else just brings burning heat, and you feel like the very life is being sucked out of you. The one secure and soothing place would be under the shadow of a great rock. What a tremendous blessing for a husband to be this place of safety, refreshing, security, and comfort for his entire family. Jesus is all four of these and a father should ask Jesus to become all four of these inside of him to his family.

CHAPTER FOUR

EIGHT COMMON PROBLEMS IN A MARRIAGE

PROBLEM NUMBER ONE: DOUBT AND UNBELIEF

God puts unbelievers in the same category as sorcerers, murderers, and whoremongers. See Revelation 21:8. Men say unbelief is a simple weakness, but God says it is an evil heart. See Hebrews 3:12. One major problem in marriage is simply believing in the power of evil to be greater than the power of almighty God. Without faith, it is impossible to please God. Anything that is not of faith is sin.

In the book of James, we read that if we pray without expecting God to answer, then we should not expect to receive anything from God because we are double-minded and unstable. Another description of unbelief is faith in the power of circumstances to overcome the power of God. If there is a real God, then he has all power, and he is able to overcome all problems that we face.

The glory of God fills the whole universe, and if we will believe God, anything is possible to us, but that is only if we will believe in God. One man came to Jesus asking him to come and pray for his daughter who was dying and Jesus said yes, but on the way, someone from his household met them and said your daughter has died. As soon as Jesus heard this he responded, "Be not afraid, only believe." See Mark 5:36.

Think of that, at the point of absolutely no hope—the girl has died—Jesus says, "only believe."

He made it sound so simple—just believe. We have received so many lies from the devil that to believe has become so complicated and hard, but to disbelieve, doubt, and analyze has become so simple!

Unbelief prevents God from doing the miraculous thing that his loving father's heart wants to do for us. When a person starts to hear all of those negative, unbelieving thoughts, like "It's hopeless," "He'll never change," "I can't love her," "I'll never be happy," or "I don't love him," all of these thoughts came with unbelief in them. Surely, unbelief is a major hindrance and problem to experiencing the fantastic marriage that God intends.

PROBLEM NUMBER TWO: TRADITIONAL VALUES

How can traditional values be a major problematic area in a marriage? If I received from my tradition the thought that all that is important to God is that I die with my marriage certificate in hand, then this can very possibly be what Peter calls an empty way of life inherited by tradition from our fathers. See 1 Peter 1:18.

If I saw my grandparents and parents stay married but no demonstration of real, authentic love, then I might think that all that matters is to stay married. It does not please God if two people do not love each other and demonstrate that love before their children and others. God is love, and he demands that we love one another. But many couples have received a lie that the most important thing is to make sure that they have their marriage certificate in their hand when they leave this world. Brothers and sisters, it is very sad if a person believes that staying married means more to God than truly loving each other. If my system of traditional values discourages me from pursuing a fantastic marriage, then these traditional values do not come from God; but instead, they distort God's heart and plan for a fantastic marriage. When children grow up in an environment where their parents display anger and take offense toward others, then these attitudes and moods become a part of the child's outlook on marriage. These children will only expect their own marriage to be a place where two people live together in disharmony and irritation and this will be seen as the normal married lifestyle.

PROBLEM NUMBER THREE: SEVERE DISAPPOINTMENTS

For twenty-six years, she carried deep fears and hidden anger. Kim (not her real name) was suffering from the effects of being kidnapped and sexually abused. Throughout most of her life, this beautiful, precious woman of God has also been carrying the deep-seated pain, grief, and sorrow of not being wanted by either her mother or father. All of these buried issues had been affecting and influencing her from the inside until the Lord brought them out to the surface. Once the wounds of these buried issues were uncovered, then the antiseptic of Christ's healing love could cleanse the infection, heal the pain, and now love can fill the space where grief, fear, and sorrow had been.

Beloved, we have prayed with many couples that have carried wounds from having experienced disappointments through each other. When a person is severely disappointed because someone that was meant to bless them abuses them or misuses them, then grief, sorrow, and pain go deep inside of their inner being. People have expectations, especially from parents, spouses, and loved ones. When these special people strongly disappoint them, something just seems to die on the inside of them. With this seeming death comes deep-seated grief and sorrow, and these same people carry this deep sorrow and grief for many years. With every future disappointment comes more sorrow, grief, and death. These issues can be extremely deep and so the person can forget that it ever happened to them. For example, every single person needs to have their earthly father to bless them. This blessing involves a total commitment to their child's destiny and well-being. It also includes words of life and love that the father speaks to his child. Also, the father's blessing gives encouragement and hope to his child that everything is going to be all right. The father's blessing brings great strength and healing to the heart of his precious child. If a fifty-year-old adult never had a father's blessing but instead he or she had an abusive father, then this adult could still be carrying a major wound that needs great healing.

Two dear men of God, seeking to please their father God, but struggled to experience the sense of the approval of the one they loved. Why did they struggle so much with experiencing God's approval? They were both in the ministry as full-time pastors. They both had precious families. They both had made many efforts to do what was pleasing to God. The reason both of them struggled with receiving God's love and acceptance was that their earthly fathers had never voiced their acceptance of them. They were constantly striving to perform in order to feel accepted, and they carried a burden to "earn their right to be alive." Many husbands can secretively carry this same burden inside of them. It becomes a driving force that is constantly working on the inside making them performance oriented. This then will also be projected onto the wife and children. A performance-oriented person is usually trying to compensate for a deep, inner wound that was put on him.

The harm that their earthly fathers had brought into them was nothing short of devastating, but the love of God came into their broken and burdened hearts and mended it. By his stripes, we are healed. Deep healing and transformation comes through the prayer of a father's blessing many times.

The way to overcome strong disappointments is to:

1. Forgive and release everyone that has strongly disappointed you, especially those who were meant to be a great blessing to you.
2. Ask God to forgive you of any judgments you might have made against them.
3. Command grief, sorrow, pain, and death to leave you and realize the actual tangible healing love of father God.

A dear sister in England realized that she was carrying the effects of being controlled and dominated by her husband. God revealed that her deep inner pain was due to many disappointments that she had been carrying for many years. Her husband's manner of speech and behavior toward her made her feel useless and like an inanimate object instead of a person. Once she realized the root causes of her deep pain and sorrow, she forgave him and released him from all disappointments. She embraced the heart of mercy and renounced the bitter heart. This resulted in her experiencing for the first time in many years peace, love and joy and her countenance revealed a woman that looked about 15 years younger. We have personally watched wrinkles disappear on a woman's face as she entered into the grace and love of Jesus. When a person carries sorrow, grief, and pain, it can result in tension on their very countenance.

PROBLEM NUMBER FOUR: DEMONIC STRONGHOLDS

Jesus said, *"I give you authority to tread on serpents, scorpions and over all the power of the enemy"* (Luke 10:19a). Jesus stated that there is one enemy. This one enemy is the devil, of whom Jesus said comes to steal, kill, and destroy. Jesus said that the devil was a liar and a murderer from the beginning. Oftentimes, the one enemy is working destruction into people's lives, and they don't even believe that he is a real being. Usually, when someone doesn't acknowledge the devil, the one who gets the blame for problems is God. People are always wondering, "Why did God allow this to happen?" Most of the time the reason God allows things to happen is to help people learn to pass the test of loving God in the midst of a temptation and to learn how to fight in the spiritual warfare that is all around.

There are two kingdoms, and they are at war. God does not have to fight the devil, but those in his kingdom do have to fight those in the kingdom of Satan. See Ephesians 6:12–17; Luke 10:19, 1 Peter 5:8–10, James 4:7; Acts 26:17–20.

Ephesians 4:27 says *that we are to give no place to the devil.* When a believer gives place to the devil through unwholesome speech, uncontrolled thoughts, or other forms of selfishness, then the devil begins to form a stronghold in his life. The main area that one must guard against in this arena of spiritual warfare is the area of thoughts. We are commanded to take every thought captive and to make each thought obey Jesus Christ. If I allow negative thoughts to enter into my mind then, they will eventually take lodging in my heart and manifest through my life in words and actions. God has said, "How long will these wicked thoughts have lodging within you." See Jeremiah 4:14b.

Some demonic strongholds, especially through ungodly, proud, self-centered thoughts cause a major problem in marriage. Any unkind thought will lead to an unkind word, and an unkind word will lead to unkind actions.

PROBLEM NUMBER FIVE: UNHEALED ISSUES

The next problem for couples is the area of unhealed issues. David said, *"Search me, O, God, and know my heart; try me and know my thoughts and see if there by any wicked way in me, and lead me in the way everlasting"* (Psalm 139:23, 24).

The word that David used for wicked actually refers to pain or toil. It apparently refers to something in David's past that caused him pain and hindered him. So often, it is the wounding experiences of our past that influences our reaction of the present. If someone wounded me by always telling me I was stupid or ugly or I will never amount to anything, this wound or tear can keep eating away at me and taking the very life out of me. *"A merry heart doeth good like a medicine; but a broken spirit drieth the bones"* (Proverbs 17:22).

The blood is in the bone marrow, and the life is in the blood; therefore, this scripture is saying that a broken spirit takes your joy of living right out of you. We were all intended to have a merry heart, but through abuse, rejection, and hatred the spirit is broken and people start to lose their joy in life. We were never meant to be hated or abused. All of this evil treatment came because of an evil one called the devil, and he put his wicked nature into man's heart in the garden.

If an individual accidentally cuts his finger it is essential for him to apply an antiseptic to prevent infection. It is the infection that can create the real danger within the body. The cut has an ability to grow new cells over it and to basically heal itself, but much danger and even amputation could result if the cut gets infected. Even so, when a person has been abused and hated, it is very important to apply the antiseptic of God's love and mercy so that no infection in the form of unforgiveness gets inside. The wound will heal if infection doesn't settle in.

Many times, if a person has been abused by a parent or an ex-spouse, then these experiences will trigger emotions and stir up old memories of hurt, rejection, and abuse. When an individual will take their hurts to the cross and forgive the ones that have abused them, ,then the blood of Jesus can and will cleanse them of all consciousness of past evils. See Hebrews 10:22.

The main condition required for this to happen is that they bring their inner wounds to Christ with a true heart of honesty about what happened to them. A dear sister in Britain had deep-seated hatred toward her father because of the abusive behavior that he displayed toward her mother. After she repented of her attitude toward her father, she received a tremendous inner healing. We have prayed with many people that created a false world within their mind. In this false, fantasy world, their parents were loving and did not hurt them at all. Unfortunately, in the real world, their mothers were abusive and unable to love and care for them. Their fathers were mean, harsh, demanding, and abusive.

In the fantasy world, there is no need for forgiveness since the parent was not abusive. But, in reality, there are many times hurt, pain, rejection, and dishonor soaked into the very memories of that individual. The main culprit that is keeping this person in bondage is the hidden judgment that they made on their parent.

PROBLEM NUMBER SIX: JUDGMENTS

The next major area of problems within a marriage is the area of unrighteous judgments. All unrighteous judgments will start to form roots of bitterness in the soul of a person. There is a biblical story in which God's people were thirsty, and they finally came to a body of water in the desert. Unfortunately, the water was bitter, and they could not drink it. The answer that the Lord gave to Moses was to throw a tree into the water and it will become sweet. See Exodus 15:25. When we go to the cross, take all of our bitter feelings to the cross, and allow the blood and mercy of God to pay the penalty for all the evil things that others did to us, then the bitter waters of life become sweet, and our heart becomes tender.

If a wife judges her husband, she will not desire to be with him, and she starts to lose her feelings of love toward him. The same thing happens when a husband judges his wife. His feelings become embittered toward her, and he'll spend less and less time in her presence. The spiritual heart is like soil, and the Word of God is a seed. The seed cannot grow where the stones occupy the space. Judgments are like stones within the soil and once the stones are removed, then the seed of the Word of God will take root and grow.

Instead of making judgments on people, we should forgive them and ask God to give them mercy. Jesus said that we were to "go and learn what that means. I will have mercy, and not sacrifice." God's will is to give mercy, and he desires that all mankind learn to love mercy and to give mercy. See Micah 6:8.

The specific way that the enemy will keep bitterness in the heart of a spouse is by constantly reminding her of what her husband said or did to her. Next, she will have the feeling that she felt when her husband said or did that to her. Next, she will have the idea that her husband needs to feel the pain or loneliness that he made her feel. Then there will be more thoughts about how he treated her. These thoughts within her heart will cause un-forgiveness, resentment, revenge, and anger to grow inside of the wife, and bitterness will become stronger and stronger. When the spouse that feels bitter and angry forgives and asks God for forgiveness for their judgments, then God will cleanse the heart, and it will once again be able to love.

The more I see my need of mercy, the more I will be able to love others and extend mercy to them. To whom much is forgiven, the same will love much. A judgmental attitude causes many problems within a marriage relationship. One lady was healed of her arthritis until she opened the door to bitterness, and then her arthritis returned. When she repented, it went away again.

PROBLEM NUMBER SEVEN: INNER VOWS

The seventh marital problem is the need to revoke all inner vows. An inner vow is a thought meditated on or spoken that is negative and against one's own life and circumstances. When a person wishes they were dead or says things like, "I will never trust a man again," this is a vow that enables evil spirits to paralyze the feelings of the heart so that she is not able to fully love another person. Whenever we say or think things that include negative, destructive wishes or words, this opens an invisible door for spirits to come in and bind us from loving and also invites death to come in and destroy the destiny of the individual.

In the tongue, God has put the power of life and the power of death. See Proverbs 18:21. The devil will take advantage of times when people say negative, destructive words. This will prevent a person from entering into the full adventure of a fantastic marriage. One must break the power of these vows by repenting and renouncing each one.

PROBLEM NUMBER EIGHT: RELYING ON SELF INSTEAD OF DEPENDING ON GOD

The last problem may be hidden for many years until finally one day we discover that all our best efforts have not worked. The first major aspect of the heart of pride says that we can of our own ability climb up the ladder of life. I can of my own ability get a better job, have a bigger ministry, have a bigger house, a better marriage, and even get to heaven of my own ability. Jesus was perfect, and he said, "I can of my own self do nothing." It is our pride that deceives us into thinking that we can of our self do anything. "We" cannot even wake up this morning unless the Lord gives us the very breath to inhale. It is the mercy of God that allowed us to wake up alive this morning. We need the mercy and grace of God to do everything. God will allow things to be going okay for a while, but then we start gloating over how well "we" are doing, then the Lord will have to allow us to start to learn about mercy and grace and how much we really depend on our Creator.

He is always there, ready to be all that an individual needs, if they will only seek him and ask for his divine assistance. Unfortunately, many times, it is not until in the midst of a crisis that it becomes clear how much the Lord was truly assisting us, but we did not know it was his grace all the time. When a person is down, it is much easier to look up. To be dependent on God alone brings a tremendous supply of the Spirit of Jesus into every marriage. He is an abundant help in time of need. He will never fail anyone that is depending on him.

All of the eight most common problems in a marriage are often the result of a wounded heart. See Proverbs 18:14 and 15:13. A wounded heart results in a crushed and wounded spirit. King David refers to the enemy persecuting his soul and wounding him.

For the enemy hath persecuted my soul; he hath smitten my life down to the ground; he hath made me to dwell in darkness, as those that have been long dead.

> *Therefore is my spirit overwhelmed within me; my heart within me is desolate.*
>
> Psalm 143:3–4

If these wounds do not receive the proper care, they will then fester into putrefying sores that have a stench in them. This is why David asked the Lord to search his heart and see if there was any wicked way in him. Isaiah said that God's people were filled with all kinds of wounds and bruises.

> *From the sole of your foot to the top of your head there is not soundness–only wounds and welts and open sores, not cleansed or bandaged or soothed with oil.*
>
> Isaiah 1:6 niv

Children are meant to be blessed and affirmed by their parents. Therefore something as seemingly insignificant as not being blessed by a mom or dad can cause a serious wound in the heart of a child. There are external sores and there are internal sores. An external sore is easy to notice, but an internal sore can go unnoticed for many years.

When external sores and cuts do not receive proper cleansing and bandaging, they can be filled with infectious pus, and every time someone touches a sore spot, it will cause further pain and irritation. Likewise, as long as a person has deep inner wounds and sores that have not been bound up, they can be compared to a city without walls. The enemy will target the sores because he knows they are where the weakest and most vulnerable places are located. It is very helpful for husbands and wives to allow the sores to be uncovered so that the Lord can come in with the cleansing and healing balm. We have seen many healed marriages once the couple allows the Lord to uncover wounds that have been buried from the past.

There is a principle behind most anger that is important to discuss at this point. A person tends to give his anger to those people that he feels would have to take it from him. For example, a man will probably not show his anger to the judge that is going to be sentencing him. Neither will a man show his anger to a police officer or his employer. A soldier in the army will probably never show his anger to the sergeant or the captain.

In ministry to troubled relationships, we have discovered many times that the present anger coming out of persons is often related to past experiences with someone who humiliated, shamed or abused him. For example, a parent makes a child feel worthless because they wet the bed or mistakenly break a glass. Innocent children can be embarrassed in front of their friends or siblings. After the humiliation, the child may feel very angry and worthless, but they will not relay their feelings to the one that caused the pain, for fear of receiving more humiliation or abuse. Now, the poison of the wound goes deeper inside of their heart. One of the main components of the spiritual heart is the inner feelings. If a nine year old boy suffered a severe disappointment, a major part of his heart could die and now his emotional growth could be stunted at nine years. Just like everyone has a physical age and their growth can be stunted, so also each person has an emotional age which can also be stunted. Therefore, a forty-five year old man could be facing life's problems with the emotional maturity of a nine year old boy. Some forty-five year old men are living with an emotional age of nine.

In the physical world, when a person cuts his arm, he needs antiseptic cleansing and stitches. If instead, the wounded person just leaves it open and dirt gets in and a scab covers the cut, it might appear to be all healed. Unfortunately, the truth will probably be that underneath the outer layer will be infectious, poisonous pus. Each time that the wound is touched, poison will be released into the body. In the natural world, for healing to take place the wound has to be re-opened so that the poison can be removed. So also, for true inner healing to take place, someone must re-open the wound and cleanse deeper where the poison has settled and then close it back up.

Stripes that wound scour away evil, and strokes (reach) the innermost parts.

Proverbs 20:30 nas

The Lord says that stripes that wound us scour away evil from inside of us. The evil that others have inflicted by wounding us is re-opened and it can feel as if we are suffering another beating. It is when this wound has been re-opened again to expose the pain and hurt, that the evil can be uncovered. The evil that others did to the wounded can now be brought to the light and the emotional pain that was buried will surface. Once this emotional pain comes to the surface, the wounded one can express in a simple prayer the way that they felt at the time of disappointment. It is at this point that many of the buried feelings of the heart will now come back and the person will start to feel again. At first, the feelings will be pain, hurt, grief, rejection, or worthlessness. Afterwards, the emotional healing can take place once the victim has forgiven the abuser and the heart can feel love, acceptance and joy in the arms of God. The Lord now comes with beauty for ashes and the oil of joy for mourning. See Isaiah 61:3. That part of the spiritual heart that had died is now alive with feeling and a sense of worth.

Now, the infection that was caused by judgments and unforgiveness is brought to the light and the individual can bring it to the cross and by his stripes they are healed. Lastly, the truth of what God's word says can replace the lies that the evil one has spoken through the one that wounded them.

It needs to be mentioned that there is one big emotional scar that many people carry with them for most of their life, and this is the wound that a sense of shame puts inside of their heart. Every child coming into the world was meant to feel that they are special; when they see their parents smiling at them, their eyes should brighten up with a sense of "I am special." If a child never sees its parents smiling at them this could easily create a sense of shame within them. Another way shame enters into a child is when expectations are placed on them in which they are not able to fulfill. For example, if a child has difficulty learning simply due to temperament and the way they were created, and if her teacher is not patient and understanding with her, she will feel ashamed or stupid. God has created each personality uniquely and special with specific learning skills. Some children are thinkers and they love to analyze problems, while others hate the process of reasoning through equations. Instead, they want to visualize and imagine and tend to be very creative and artistic. If we do not allow people to be who God made them to be, then we can shame them into feeling guilty about how God made them. There are many innocent adults that have suffered shame because they could not fulfill some expectation from an authority figure. Maybe they were not athletic, did not get good grades, or did not accomplish the achievements of an older sibling. I am encountering more and more people that carry deep-seated shame inside of them. They feel that they are stupid or a failure or will never amount to anything. Often, these dear individuals are very special and they have tender hearts and are sensitive to suffering in others. Their own sufferings have somehow allowed them to feel for others who suffer. Once the person allows the Lord to heal the wound of shame inside of them, then they are able to love more deeply and feel their worth and value in life.

CHAPTER FIVE

THE PLACE OF HONOR IN THE HOME

Honor all men. Love the brotherhood. Fear God. Honor the King.
1 Peter 2:17

In this section, we will study about honor. God has commanded us to honor all men. Some definitions of honor would include official dignity, repute, esteem, high regard, or great respect given, received, or enjoyed. The biblical meaning of the word for honor is to prize; to fix a valuation upon; by implication to revere; to estimate, to fix the value. More meanings of this word for honor are of great price, precious, held for honor, esteemed, and especially dear. To honor all men is to esteem them in your heart as a person that has great value because God is the Father of their spirit, and therefore, they are an eternal being with an eternal destiny. See Numbers 16:22 and 27:16, Hebrews 12:9.

The psalmist declares that God has crowned mankind with glory and honor. The very nature of God is filled with an understanding of honor and blessing. If someone really enters into God's heart, he will go deep into the very concepts of honor.

The entire concept of dishonor is to be discovered in the very heart and nature of Satan. There are many deep hidden attitudes of dishonor and disrespect in the heart of a person that abuses and mistreats another individual. If someone truly bestowed honor on another human being, it would be almost impossible to do any harm or damage to that one.

TYPES OF HONOR

There are different types of honor. One type of honor is the kind that you achieve or earn such as winning a game or godly character. Another kind of honor is the kind you are to be given due to your status in life such as a president, a professor, a bishop, or a parent. A position of leadership entitles a person to honor. In the church, an elder who labors in the Word is worthy of double honor. See 1 Timothy 5:17.

Wives are to receive a special type of honor due to two reasons: 1) they are a fellow heir to the grace of life. In other words, my wife is not only my wife, but also my sister in the Lord. 2) She is the weaker vessel and there-fore husbands are to give their wives a special honor. God always bestows more honor on weaker things.

In the body of Christ, the Holy Spirit wants the less honorable and weaker members of the body to receive more abundant honor so that no member feels left out and no member receives the main recognition but that the whole body is recognized. When the greater gives more honor to the lesser, then the body is being seen as one new man, and the entire body gets the whole focus and not any particular member.

In the church, there are some members that receive much greater recognition than others, and Paul refers to this as schism in the body. The Holy Spirit says that Christians are to give more abundant honor to the ones who feel like their place in the church is not as important. In the same way wives are to be given more honor because they are the weaker vessel. It is not lesser but weaker. There is no shame in being the weaker vessel, and God will show his perfect power in my weakness. God has chosen the weak things to confound the things that are strong. If a husband does not show honor to his wife, then his prayers will be cut off by God. God will not hear a husband's prayers that does not show and give honor to his wife. See 1 Peter 3:7.

What does it mean for a husband to give honor to his wife? This refers to showing by demonstration to the family and to others that his wife is valuable and she is special. This would mean that it would never be appropriate for a husband to put down or to joke about his wife because this could reveal to the listeners an attitude that my wife is not valuable and she is just a joke.

The Holy Spirit has been very strict with me regarding not saying any words to my wife in private or public that would make her feel stupid, silly, or bad about herself. Since wives are the weaker vessel, they need to be given words that would encourage, edify, and empower them to fulfill their destiny in life. God has put strength in the soul of a man to sustain the wife in the midst of emotional upheaval. If a man is emotionally unstable, this may have serious effects on the couple when pressures are great and trials are seemingly unending in a marriage.

Children should behold as dad shows the preciousness of their mother to them. Mom should also display honor to her husband as a human being made to display God's very image. Parents should let their children feel that they also are valuable by giving honor to them. One great need in many cultures today is the need to honor old age. It is so easy to forget the sacrifices that the elderly have made so that the younger generation can enjoy many blessings and privileges. Psalm 112 describes how God has promised to make an offspring greatly blessed and mighty in this world due to their father's love for God and delight in his ways.

DISHONOR DESTROYS BUT HONOR HEALS

Due to dishonor and selfishness, many times children do not realize the extent that their parents have suffered for them so that they could be blessed. Any loving parent will make sacrifices for their children with great delight. Children need to show honor to their parents no matter what their parent's character might be. If a parent has evil characteristics, it is still the responsibility of the child to honor their parent. This honor reflects that the child values his parent because they are created by God with a tremendous destiny and purpose. This does not imply that children should always obey their parents. If a parent wants a child to do something evil in God's sight, then this child must obey God and not their parent. No man can serve two masters. Children should always have an attitude on the inside of their heart that gives honor to their parents. It is not only possible, but also helpful to learn to give honor to people whose lives are wrecked by evil. The reason for this is: it is almost for certain that these wrecked lives would not be wrecked if others would have given them honor in their past. When a child shows honor to an abusive parent, he or she is communicating that I still love you and forgive you and I realize that the way your life has turned out is not the way that God intended, but you still have value and you can still find mercy with God.

If a person takes a $3 million diamond and throws it into the garbage heap, it is still worth $3 million. Just because someone has made choices to destroy their precious life, does not mean that their life is no longer precious. The value of the life is given by the Creator of that life. God has made a wonderful creation, and as we all learn to love and honor his creation, we will start to believe that he has far more power to redeem that life than the power of the devil to destroy it. The more we give honor to each other, the more God will heal deep inner hurts, and the more we dishonor one another, the more we will destroy one another.

If in-laws or grandparents live in a home, then this entire family should bestow honor on each and every member. If honor would saturate every inch within a home, then there would be very little interferences with in-laws. There would be no hate or jealousy, and the atmosphere would be charged with kindness, appreciation, and love. How extremely precious would the family become if each and every member saw each other as a person that deserved to be treated with honor. Never could a man rape someone he honored. Never could a man hate someone he honored. Never could a man kill someone he honored. Never could a man abuse, neglect, or abandon someone he honored. Social, economic, and political injustice would be practically nonexistent in the midst of the society and culture that obeyed the Lord by "giving honor to all men."

Some specific ways that a person can give honor to another is to listen to them while they are speaking. Another way to give honor is to pay attention and have a good posture while they are speaking. A person's attitude is revealed by his posture and facial expression while in the presence of others. If there is honor toward another within my heart, then it will come out in kind words, thoughtful feelings, a listening ear, and an affectionate touch.

One very important way to honor is to speak blessings over that one. Right after the Lord created mankind, he blessed them.

So God created man in his own image, in the image of God created he him; male and female created he them. And God blessed them, and God said unto them, Be fruitful, and multiply, and replenish the earth, and subdue it: and have dominion over the fish of the sea, and over the fowl of the air, and over every living thing that moveth upon the earth.

Genesis 1:27, 28

Jesus would go out of his way to put his hands on children and bless them.

And they brought young children to him, that he should touch them: and his disciples rebuked those that brought them. But when Jesus saw it, he was much displeased, and said unto them, Suffer the little children to come unto me, and forbid them not: for of such is the kingdom of God. Verily I say unto you, Whosoever shall not receive the kingdom of God as a little child, he shall not enter therein. And he took them up in his arms, put his hands upon them, and blessed them.

Mark 10:13–16

The last thing that Jesus did while he was on earth was to bless his disciples.

And he led them out as far as to Bethany, and he lifted up his hands, and blessed them.

Luke 24:50

God has declared that there is tremendous power in our speech. There is the power of life and death in the tongue. See Proverbs 18:21. There are two main ways to bless our family: touch and speech. A gentle and kind touch can communicate volumes to an individual. It can make them feel special; it can tell them, "I like to be near you," and, "I love you." Touch is so essential to well-being that there is a specific neurotic condition that is basically the result of not being touched, and this is called deprivation neurosis. It has been researched that children suffer great harm when they are not touched. When a child is touched in an inappropriate way, this can cause even greater harm. All human beings want to be touched, and everyone needs to be loved. Another way to give honor to your family, especially your spouse, is to speak blessings over them. Throughout the day, a wife can speak blessings over her husband. Instead of thinking on how many wrongs are in his life, she can start to speak blessings over those areas where he might be deficient or weak. One woman started to bless her body after she repented for all the negative things that she had previously spoken over her body. Within several weeks, she had lost over twenty pounds. Truly, God has given us great power to bless each other, *"not returning evil for evil, or insult for insult, but giving blessing instead; for you were called for the very purpose that you might inherit a blessing"* (1 Peter 3:9, nas).

While a spouse is sleeping, the other one can speak blessings. What a wonderful time for a husband to put his hand on his wife and bless her. If we do not control our speech, we could easily dishonor our spouse and release the power of death through our lips! Or we could use the power of speech to release life and give special honor to our beloved mate. It is the desire of almighty God to use each one of us to impart blessings to his creatures, but we must be committed to being an instrument of his peace. One last word: there is an evil one that desires to use our lips to release curses to God's creatures. Each human being has to decide which spirit will use his lips: the Holy Spirit or the evil spirit. May we not underestimate the blessing or harm that our speech can and does cause others?

Oh, beloved, it is time to see God's creation through the eyes of the Creator himself. May honor begin in the husband for the wife and then multiply through the family and to the parents, grandparents, relatives, and then to all creation. Then shall the commandment of almighty God find fulfillment and his word to show honor to all men become a reality. Men are called to be leaders in society, and one area that men need to demonstrate leadership is in the area of giving honor to all people.

CHAPTER SIX

ENEMIES OF A PRIEST AND KING

And hath made us kings and priests unto God and his Father, to him be glory and dominion forever and ever. Amen.
Revelation 1:6

We are called to be priests and kings in Christ to God the Father. It is especially true that in a home a man is called to be a leader, priest, and king. First, he is to be a priest and king to God, and then he is called to be a priest and king to his family. There is a high calling in Christ Jesus for every man. When a person submits to the control and authority of Jesus Christ, then the High Priest and Apostle himself will equip this man with the nature and authority to be a priest and king.

In order to be a priest, one must have a heart full of compassion for the people. See Hebrews 5:2.7

To be a king a person must use authority to have dominion over the area under his power and jurisdiction. The two enemies of being a priest and king are anger and passivity.

THE ENEMY OF A PRIEST: SELFISH ANGER

All forms of selfish anger are cursed by God.

> *Simeon and Levi are brethren; instruments of cruelty are in their dwelling place. O my soul, come not thou into their secret; mine honour, be not thou united: for in their anger they slew a man and in their self-will they hamstrung an ox. Cursed be their anger, for it is fierce; And their wrath, for it is cruel!*
>
> Genesis 49:5–7

Simeon and Levi had a mother that was hated by her husband. The evil one loves to disperse his vicious hate into our descendants. Simeon and Levi had anger, and God said that it was cursed. All self-centered anger is cursed because it does not consider the needs or feelings of others. This selfish anger will show hostility to people that conflict with its own selfish desires.

If a child lives in an environment of angry people, he will have to overcome this anger and receive God's love within his heart. God will visit the iniquity of the fathers on the children. See Exodus 20:5b. Therefore, when a person tolerates selfish anger in his heart, his family will suffer the consequence of his iniquity. Many times children will inherit traits from their ancestors such as: eye color, hair texture, propensities to physical disease and the very genetic code. Apparently, sinful tendencies can also be passed to children. God says whatever a man sows, this shall he also reap. See Galatians 6:7. Anger has a way of infecting many people with its poison. For example, if a parent disciplines his child in harsh anger, this will reap destruction in the heart of his child. On the other hand, when a parent disciplines his child in love, this will reap life and strength in the child. David attributed his personal greatness to God's gentleness. A father and husband can have a specific form of anger that is directed towards weakness. This type of anger can damage the soul of the wife and children. This father might think that his disposition is for the good of his family, but it could be creating fear, self-hatred and rejection. We should ask ourselves the question "have we assimilated the mean hard attitudes of our ancestors, or are we exercising godly discipline in love?" When a person has been conditioned by an atmosphere of anger, this anger can become an inner force that drives him to achieve, conquer and to succeed. This will result in this person becoming a very driven individual lacking peace and joy. Jesus said "my peace do I give unto you" (see John 16:33 and 20:21).

Jesus was very active. He accomplished great things, and he lived his entire life in perfect peace. A young man can have buried memories of how his earthly dad abused and dominated him. He may be internally driven for years to show his dad that he will amount to something because he never received his father's encouragement and blessing. Therefore, most of this man's life will be lived in tension and anxiety while he is trying to perform in order to be accepted. The whole inner structure working in this man's very thought patterns create a deep-seated frustration within his being.

Dan (name changed) was a very successful businessman, but he was very tense and full of frustration due to his internal need to feel accepted and to feel special in life. Dan's father was a harsh demanding and unfeeling person, and often he would make Dan feel stupid and inferior to him. Eventually, Dan learned to see himself as an incapable little boy, even in his older adult years. Dan's deep inner sense of failure and incompetence made him a very tense and angry person. His frustration would be given to his innocent wife and family. Once Dan forgave his earthly father and released him from all the pain, rejection, and emotional abuse that he caused him; then Dan was released, cleansed, and freed from the deep inner feeling of anger and disappointment that had controlled his life. Now, Dan's life is characterized by peace and joy, and he shows his wife and family love and appreciation, but first, he had to find love and appreciation for himself as a man.

Once again it needs to be mentioned that sometimes a man receives a specific form of hatred and this is toward women, in which there is no real cause other than the fact that she is a woman. This deep-seated, frustrated anger is not only directed toward women, but it is many times released when people demonstrate signs of weakness. This anger is usually passed down through the father's generational line; therefore, a man that has this type of anger probably had a grandfather that was mean, demanding, harsh, and controlling toward his grandmother. Also, this man would have witnessed much of the same harsh behavior through his father toward his mother. Many harsh, demanding men are perpetrators of this form of hatred toward the females and toward weakness in general. To these men they interpret slowness, shyness, and fear as a demonstration of weakness. One thing must be emphasized at this point: this hatred can have an outward appearance of niceness, but it will cause a woman or girl to feel as if she has just been cut inwardly. This is probably what David was referring to in Psalm 55:21. His speech was smoother than butter, but in his heart was war; his words were softer than oil, yet they were drawn swords. It must be also borne in mind that when a person reacts in judgment and bitterness, then this same evil that we judge in another now has the legal power to come into the person that made the judgment. So, if a father did not have sons to pass this hatred to, then if his daughter judged him, she will probably grow up as a mom with much of the same anger and hate toward girls and toward weakness.

I have traveled to parts of the world where women seem to have this form of anger. It is a wonderful sight to see the Lord heal and deliver many people from this deep-seated anger. We have also seen how children who have been victims of this sort of anger from their mothers have been helped See 1 John 3:12. All selfish anger comes from the evil one.

Billy (name changed) was married to Rhoda (name changed) for over thirty years. One day Bill was delivered from hatred towards women. The next morning Bill and Rhoda went to a store just to walk around and do a little shopping. While they were walking in the store, and holding hands, Rhoda had an overwhelming sense of love from Bill. She felt like she was on her honeymoon. For the first time in her life, she felt like she was "covered" by Bill. She felt safe, secure, and special just walking around the store and holding Bill's hand. The misogyny (hatred of women) had so dominated Bill's life that he didn't even realize that he was uncovering his dear wife all these years. This hatred that had operated in his heart was passed down through Bill's grandfather who was a preacher. Bill's ancestry had many individuals who were mentally ill, murderers, depressed, suicidal, drug addicts, alcoholics and much rebellion. Whatever a man sows, this shall he also reap.

Although Bill's grandfather, like so many other Christian men, really loved the Lord, apparently he did not realize that he had this hatred toward women. This inner hatred usually causes a person to be insensitive, harsh, short-tempered, demanding, and impatient with their spouse or a weaker vessel. All of these sinful tendencies and abusive lifestyles were a by-product of deep inner hatred toward women. How very sad that a man can call himself a Christian but deep inside of his own heart still harbor these kinds of attitudes of anger and frustration toward his own precious, innocent loved ones. Beloved, our Christianity must begin at home with those people closest to us. The Holy Spirit will always convict us of any attitudes that grieve him and this includes any mean, unkind word that we speak to our spouses. If we will just ask ourselves the question, "Where did that evil, harsh word that just came out of my mouth come from?" Then, the Holy Spirit will reveal the source of that hatred. It will always have its source in the nature of Satan, which is pride, but it will often come down to us through an ancestor and even possibly through a grandfather that was a preacher. Also, it is not good for any minister to speak a derogatory word from his pulpit toward his wife.

If a husband has this anger and he is a churchgoer, then he will probably cover it with charm and nice words while in the presence of other Christians. If he is not a churchgoer, then he will probably show his hostility toward his wife in the presence of others. Many times his friends and buddies are unkind toward their spouses, and this causes the hidden hatred to go undetected when they are all together. Therefore, it remains a hidden, evil fire burning in the heart of this dear husband because he does not see any visible sign of how wives should be treated by their husbands. It is extremely important for men to see a godly example of how a husband should be toward his wife. It is my prayer that many men who read this book will become these examples to other husbands and another holy fire will start to burn inside of them.

Some of the roots that keep this person bound are fear of being abandoned, shame, and rage. This rage can be like a fire inside of the wounded heart of this person. This type of anger or rage will prevent a person from showing compassion as a priest should to others. This anger will despise others, especially if they are female and if they are going slow and showing signs of weakness. These people generally will boast inside their heart about their achievements and successes in which they have accomplished in life. Their pride in their achievements is the main source of their condemnation of others. They have learned to lift themselves up in pride, and this has resulted in putting others down (this all takes place on the inside of a person's heart).

Often when a husband has this hatred inside, his wife will feel uncovered and vulnerable to fear, self-hatred, and rejection. Instead of being the leader in humility, strength, kindness, and love, this man becomes a demanding dictator to his dear wife. A wife will respond in one of two ways to the abusive harsh anger of her husband, and this is determined mostly by her personality type. First, if their temperament or personality is more on the weak and quiet side, she will probably respond in great fear and behave like a beaten animal. Secondly, if her temperament is on the strong and verbal side, she will retaliate with anger and harshness. Either reaction will cause frustration, tension, and unrest in the home and will open the door wider to the devil to work destruction in the marriage.

Jesus is the head of the church, which is his spiritual body on earth. May the kindness of the head start to fill his entire body on earth, when this happens, many marriages will be healed as leaders (men) ask forgiveness and take the blame for their ungodly attitudes and actions. Then this power of kindness will be ignited into the hearts of children and other believers and throughout the body of Christ.

To overcome this anger, one must renounce all forms of hatred that was tolerated by his ancestors and forgive them for their sins. See John 20:23. Next, he must release everyone that made him feel ashamed and hurt him in any way. Thirdly, he must ask forgiveness for any judgments he made on his father or on any woman. Fourthly, he must command any spirits of anger to leave him and break any effects on his mind or emotions that they have exerted over him. Lastly, he must ask Jesus to love his wife and children through him. Now is the time to see women and people and their weaknesses the way Jesus Christ sees them. Jesus will start to look through our eyes, and we will see people the way he sees them. Women that have suffered from these abusive heart attitudes from men, whether they were fathers, brothers, husbands or ministers, are usually always in need of inner healing and deliverance, especially from self-hatred, bitterness, fear, and a deep sense of hopelessness and uselessness. These wounded women feel very discouraged and hurt because deep down their spirit realizes that they did not deserve this type of treatment from the very ones called by God to lead and love them into wholeness.

THE ENEMY OF A KING: PASSIVITY

The second enemy that will prevent a person from being a king is passivity. Oftentimes, a child will be ashamed and fearful because something negative happened in his life or family, and then he assimilates fear and shame into his personality. He has two choices at this point: 1) control his environment so that he will not have to face his fears and shame; 2) in honesty, come to the truth regarding the shame and fear that has entered into his personality. A person can be timid and controlling at the very same time. For example, if a person fears confrontation, he can then learn to avoid it by arranging his circumstances in such a way that he is in control. He may have fifty employees that are all under him or he may have a job in which he is totally isolated from other people. Shyness or timidity can be an open doorway for a spirit of passivity to enter a person's life. One of the best examples in the Bible of a man with a spirit of passivity is Lot. Passivity is the refusal to make proper choices. This, in turn, opens an invisible doorway to a force that will debilitate and weaken a person so that he will not be able to overcome in the spiritual arena of battle.

- A passive man will not be able to exercise his authority to rule as a king.
- A passive man will be weakened in the area of his will.
- A passive man will be tormented by the evil around him instead of manifesting the light of Christ into the darkness; he allows his righteous soul to be tormented by the darkness. See 2 Peter 2:8, Ephesians 5:13.
- A passive man will give his loved ones over to the forces of darkness all around him. See Genesis 19:8 (un-godly television, certain types of music, etc.).
- A passive man will be moved by what his eyes see and his ears hear. See Genesis 13:10, 11. He will make choices based on natural circumstances instead of listening to the voice of God.
- A passive man will not be taken seriously by those close to him, even in times of crisis; they will not heed his voice. See Genesis 19:14. His normal behavior often has joking, and therefore, his family does not perceive the seriousness of the situation in times of crisis. Possibly, under the surface, people look at him as a joker, and so they do not respect his power to lead in spiritual conflict and he is not seen as a man of prayer. Many times a man bound by passivity is not a man of prayer.
- A passive man will not be able to surrender everything into God's hands even in the midst of impending immediate doom. See Genesis 19:16.
- A passive man will not make necessary choices, and therefore, others will have to take the role of a leader in his place. See Joshua 24:14, 15, Judges 4:7–9.

- Lastly, a man with passivity lives in fear and shame. A spirit of passivity will prevent a man from being the warrior and leader of his family that he is called to be. The wife of a man with passivity gets overwhelmed with the sense of responsibility that she is left to handle because of her husband's fear of making a mistake. He will procrastinate in many areas and not make important decisions for fear of making the wrong choices. He is often enslaved by the fear of failure. Just a normal comment made by his wife is taken as an attack of his very person and rejection sets in.

Two men in their twenties were both set free from a spirit of passivity one day. Jim (not his real name) was never able to take exams. He always felt fear and bondage in the area of education. After his deliverance, he went to school, received extremely high grades, and graduated in a short time within a difficult field of study. He noticed there was no longer the bondage of taking exams and fearing the outcome. Next, Bob (not his real name) was always held back in life by the fear of making choices, but after his deliverance from passivity, he can now take the lead as a father and husband, and now there are many areas in his life that no longer hold him back.

What keeps passivity in a person's life is the cycle of pride, fear, shame, and control. As long as a man tries to control his life and does not come to the truth of his fear and shame, this passivity will continue to dominate his life. Some doorways that could have allowed passivity to enter a person are:

- Shyness and timidity as a child. Webster's Dictionary defines shyness as "being uncomfortable in the presence of and avoiding contact with others, extremely self-conscious."
- Being told what to do all the time by a parent.
- Repeated refusal to make choices.

- A blank mind (instead of making personal choices, others use their power to choose for you). This is a form of witchcraft, and the enemy loves for someone or something like drugs to cause our mind to become blank.
- People that speak words into you, such as "he's shy," "he's bashful," "she's so quiet," "she never does anything." All these words open an invisible doorway for passivity and it starts to influence their personality.

As time goes on, a person will descend deeper and deeper into a pit of passivity unless he starts to overcome the feelings of fear and shame and decides to humble himself and to seek help out of his pit.

OPPOSITES ATTRACT

A man with passivity will get involved with a woman that is very strong-willed. This is due to the fact that deep inside of this man, he really desires to not be so passive, and he likes the active, non-passive attitude of the woman he is with. A man does not like his passivity any more than a drug addict likes his addiction. Men are meant to be warriors. This is why little boys usually like playing with guns and fighting.

Now, a person can break agreement with the spirit of passivity and command its power broken over his life. After a person has repented of giving ground to passivity, now he can take authority over it and ask the Lord to strengthen him in every area where his will has been weakened. See Isaiah 14:12c, Ephesians 3:16. It is also important for a person with passivity to release all the people who caused him to be fearful and ashamed. In every one of these areas, it is important to deal with all malice and ill feelings by forgiving the people involved and by releasing everyone that caused the pain and sorrow through disappointment, rejection, and betrayal.

People find themselves bound in an area of hurt because they have been focusing only on what the other person did to them and totally ignoring their response to that person. If someone abused me and I judged them and harbor malice toward them in my heart, then I am in prison, and I am just as guilty in God's sight as the offender. Jesus said that everything that causes offense and makes people to stumble must be removed from his kingdom.

In conclusion, a husband that is bound by passivity must see his need to be free, and he must understand how frustrating it is for a wife to be dependent on a leader who is refusing to lead. Next, we will study the role of the wife in a marriage relationship.

CHAPTER SEVEN

THE ROLE OF THE WOMAN IN A MARRIAGE

The woman was taken out of man; therefore, she is carrying a part of man that is needed for the man to be complete. Since it is not good for a man to be alone, it's "good" for a woman to be with him. A woman is not to take leadership over a man, but she is an extremely vital part in a godly leader's life. Her part is to come under a man's godly leadership and to support him in his infirmities and deficiencies. If a man does not want to take the leadership, then God will find a woman to take his place, but God's highest is to find "seven men" full of the Holy Ghost and wisdom and of honest report. See Acts 6:3. God's plan has always been that men would be leaders.

There is responsibility and order even in the Godhead. Jesus said that, "the Father is greater than I" (John 14:28).

There is order in the very universe because God is a God of order. Satan creates disorder, disease, and disharmony. It is very beneficial when a wife learns to submit to her husband with a meek and quiet spirit. This is one of the few things mentioned as extremely precious in the sight of God.

Sarah obeyed her godly husband Abraham and even called him lord. This beautiful heart in Sarah brought great blessings to her and to her family. God views this attitude of heart as extremely valuable. There seems to be two extremes today in Christian theology regarding the role of women.

1. Wives must submit and obey no matter what the husband says.
2. Wives are free in Christ to do whatever they feel the Holy Spirit is telling them to do.

The first extreme takes away the individuality of the woman, and the second one gives total supremacy to the individuality of the woman. Both of these extremes ignore the major importance of the inner attitude in the heart of the woman. For example, the Word of God declares that the wife holds a tremendous power within her. This can be used to the glory of God and his kingdom and to the edifying of godly leadership, or this tremendous power can be misused and abused by women to her own selfish desires and pleasures.

If a man, because of his selfish pride, believes that he can be a great success without his helpmate, then he is greatly deceived. It is possible he could abuse and ignore the very one that could make him a success and bring a completion and a fullness to his life.

Also, men in our world are so dependent on women that women can use this to their advantage. Men likewise can use their money, power, and force to dominate women and control them. Some women, although, will fight with their own power that God has put in them, and they will start to advance in the empires of this present world. This is why God states, "a virtuous woman, who can find?" (Proverbs 31:10).

There is such a God ordained dependence of the man on the woman that the more mankind drifts away from the importance of the woman, the more he will become confused about his own importance. There could never be a man if he did not come into the world through the channel of a woman.

"Her price is far above rubies." In other words, a real godly woman will bring much more success and wealth into a man's life than rubies could. Rubies could increase his finances, but a virtuous woman will increase and multiply many helpful qualities within the life of a man. She is worth far more than rubies because the power she holds is much greater than the power of rubies. There are a multitude of benefits that a virtuous woman brings into a family. The following are ten benefits of a virtuous woman.

1. Her husband's heart trusts fully in her, and he feels safe from any betrayal.
2. Her husband is only profited and not hurt by her all the days of her life.
3. Her husband is known with the leaders of the city, and those in high government places respect him.
4. Her husband and family receive her wisdom and are blessed by her kind words.
5. She discerns the needs of her family and helps to meet them.
6. Her children stand up to express that their mother is a blessed woman of God.
7. Her husband also declares that his wife is godly and to be praised greatly.
8. She sees the deceit of the approval of man.
9. She knows the uselessness and vanity of outward beauty only.
10. She lives her life from the heart, and she desires to fear God. Therefore, she lives to please him, and God will take notice one day and give her praise.

All these ten qualities of a virtuous godly woman are described in Proverbs 31.

This godly, virtuous woman is very hard to find, but when she is found, she will be a major reason that God has used to create a fantastic marriage. This woman will reveal the beautiful and lovely, lowly bride of Christ, and the world will see her and desire her exquisite radiance. She will realize her inner beauty is the very beauty of the Lord himself in her. See Ezekiel 16:14.

The role of the woman is to submit and this submission acts as a support so that her husband may stand upon her undergirding and trust. Next, the husband will now find an additional strength and satisfaction in fulfilling his purpose and calling to be a godly leader. The Lord showed me once that when a wife voices her disapproval for an area in her husband's life, sometimes this is an area that he has been trying to overcome, and when she speaks out against it, she takes the very support that he was relying on out from under him, and it causes him to want to give up or be discouraged. Most often, a man really desires to change in an area in his life, but he needs help to overcome, and God will use his helpmate to pray and intercede for him until he overcomes.

May the Lord open the eyes of every man to see the worth, beauty, and power that every woman has to complement and complete him. May every woman also see the glory of what God has given her, her worth, her calling, and power, and may she not despise it or abuse it. Lastly, may every woman that has been raped, dishonored, abused, and treated like dirt please forgive and release every person that has done this to you. May you allow the Lord to heal and restore your honor and influence in this world because you are so much needed.

CHAPTER EIGHT

THE MANIFEST PRESENCE (THE GREATEST SECRET)

If this entire book was read and this one chapter was left out, then this book would be of little or no worth. The only way to a fantastic marriage is through the one who has declared Himself to be the way, the truth, and the life. This chapter is about the manifest presence and not the omnipresence. The omnipresence is the fact that the presence of God is everywhere, every moment of every day.

God's presence pervades all of his creation, but there are only certain times that the omnipresent Lord chooses to reveal or manifest his presence to the consciousness of people. It is at these times in which the Lord reveals himself to individuals that individuals are greatly impacted and the hearts of people are changed. Jesus said, *"He that hath my commandments, and keepeth them, he it is that loveth me: and he that loveth me shall be loved of my Father, and I will love him, and will manifest myself to him"* (John 14:21).

Jesus mentioned to his disciples that the Holy Spirit will glorify him. "He shall glorify me; for he shall receive of mine, and shall show it unto you" (see John 16:14). So, it is the Holy Spirit that honors and reveals Christ to his disciples.

> *And his name shall be called Wonderful, Counselor, the Mighty God, the Everlasting Father; the Prince of Peace.*
>
> Isaiah 9:6b

When the Bible mentions God's name, it is almost always making reference to his very nature. So, when the Lord manifests himself to people, he is revealing who and what he is. He is Wonderful (full of wonder). He is Counselor (full of wisdom). He is the Mighty God (full of power). He is the Everlasting Father (full of Father's heart of mercy and love). He is Prince of Peace (full of perfect peace). When Jesus chooses to manifest his presence, all of his wonder, wisdom, power, love, and peace will also emerge in accordance with what is the most needed at the time for the individual. The above five aspects of the nature of Christ is all sufficient and complete. Jesus doesn't show us the way: he is the way. Jesus doesn't give us truth: he is the truth. Jesus doesn't let us have some life: he is the life. His presence within a couple is all that the couple will need. He will be their wonder, he will be their wisdom, he will be their might, he will be their love, he will be their peace, and he himself will be all that they need.

David said in his presence was fullness of joy and at his right hand are pleasures forevermore. See Psalm 16:11.

WHAT HAPPENS WHEN JESUS WALKS INTO THE ROOM?

Jesus' manifest presence will cause things to take place in a family. He will soften hard hearts. His lovely presence will turn the rock into a pool of water. The hard unyielding places in the heart will melt. Many times in our family, the manifest presence of Jesus has come and our wonderful Lord broke the hardness that was starting to form within and washed our hearts clean. His presence has been the major secret of keeping our hearts soft and tender.

His presence brings great joy and delight as long as someone is trying to please him. His presence brings light and the hidden places of darkness are exposed. Family members are convicted of sin, wrong thoughts, and selfish motives of the heart are revealed.

His presence will fill the home with a deep, deep peace, even in the midst of opposition and confusion from the outside pressures of life's problems. The presence of Christ will calm the storms of life. He will make the troubled waters to cease and everything will be peaceful as long as Jesus is in our boat in the midst of the storm. See Matthew 8:24 and Matthew 14:24–26.

His beautiful presence will bring a beauty and a sweetness that will fill hearts with a deep sense of awe and splendor.

His presence will always resist the presence of pride, envy and hatred.

His presence will bring healing to the body and to the soul of each family member.

Jesus has risen from the dead ,and through the Holy Spirit, Jesus comes to live inside of us. Therefore, Jesus wants to walk with each person. He desires to carry their burdens and to be a vital part of their daily life. He is a real person that has promised he will never leave us or forsake us. If individuals will sincerely ask the Lord Jesus to live in them and to walk amongst them, then he will reveal himself to them.

His presence will quicken the mortal body with energy and strength. See Romans 8:11.

When the Lord reveals his mighty presence, somehow everyone realizes that everything is going to work out. He brings a deep settled confidence that he governs all. See Psalms 22:28.

In the presence of Christ, love conquers all forms of hate.

Lastly, in his wonderful presence, the inner eye of the heart is opened to see the pride on the inside and also to see the great compassion within the heart of God.

The greatest secret of a fantastic marriage is to have the magnificent Lord Jesus to come so near to each spouse that they lose all consciousness of self and have no more remaining need to be self-centered. In the beauty of his holy presence, there is only one supreme desire, and this is to please him in every thought, word, and deed. The manifest presence brings a great longing within an individual to love and please God in everything. As an individual pleases God, they now become the most kind, the most gentle, and the most loving individual to live with. Their heart becomes one with the heart of the lamb, and his heart is meek and lowly. Moses spent so much time in the manifest presence of God that he became the meekest man on earth. The one consuming passion of King David was to behold the beauty of the Lord in his presence all the days of his life. See Psalm 27:4. This desire consumed David's heart, and God said David was a man after his own heart.

If a husband and wife make worship their highest goal and they both long for the manifest presence in their marriage, then their marriage can only become a fantastic marriage burned within their hearts and maintained by the very fire of God's heart, which is a furnace of burning love.

One of God's names is everlasting burnings and devouring fire. When two individuals become one with him whose name is everlasting burnings, they will be filled with the very passion of God's own heart. This cannot be anything less than a fantastic marriage filled with fire and burning with pure love. May we not be satisfied with a mediocre or even a good marriage. May we receive what God is offering each couple—an abundant life full of His love. See Ephesians 3:17–20.

If we really desire a fantastic marriage, then we must learn to love the fire. Fire equals fantastic in a marriage. A fire goes before him and burns up all of his enemies. The fire of God's consuming love will burn out of us all that is an enemy to us having a fantastic marriage.

CHAPTER NINE

LOVING YOUR SPOUSE'S GOD-GIVEN TEMPERAMENT

In 1977, Marie and I started to date. I loved her 90 lb. frame, the braces on her teeth and short hair. I thought to myself, "I really like this girl." So, our relationship had begun and we started to be together more often. Growing up in my family, everyone had something to say and if you didn't express your opinion quick enough, then you would simply listen to others speak their mind. Needless to say, there was plenty of open communication and people sharing their thoughts continuously. This process became very natural for me. We all voiced our opinions about life on a regular basis. In Marie's family if her father was at home, than he would do much of the talking and Marie was always very quiet.

My new girlfriend and I would go out together and share time with one another. I began speaking to Marie and expected to have an open and easy flow of communication between us. I would often share my thoughts and then ask the question, "What do you think?" or "Where would you like to go?". I would anxiously wait for my sweetheart to respond to my simple question. However I did not get the response I expected. Marie would say very quietly "I don't know," "nothing," "anywhere," or she would not have anything at all to respond. This caused a reaction inside of my heart. I could not believe that she would not answer my simple question. So, I would usually repeat my question; but the second time, I would ask with a little frustration in my tone of voice. As a result of my repeated questioning, and frustrated tone, her answer became less and less, and she would say nothing at all. My beautiful sweetheart started to look different to me at this point. She was not as beautiful anymore and I started to seriously wonder, "What is her problem?".

There are so many truths that I didn't known back then, but now; thirty-six years later I can say that I have learned a lot. I would like to share with my readers some of the truths that were working in me during this time 36 years ago.

I thought that my temperament was the best; therefore I looked down on the wonderful way that God had made Marie.

I had judged Marie for her lack of response. (Please read my book called, "The Key to Staying in Love").

Due to my frustration with Marie, I was causing her to go inside of a shell, where she could feel safe; instead of talking to a frustrated, proud boyfriend.

My temperament was outward, open and did not fear pressure; but instead almost welcomed it as a tool for debate.

Marie's temperament did not respond quickly and it does not like pressure. When someone puts pressure on this temperament, they turn inward and shut down. In other words, I was the main cause for my sweetheart's lack of response.

Marie and I both had baggage from our past and with God's help, we would learn how to entrust our baggage into the care of the baggage keeper (1Samuel 17:22).

One of the first Christian books that I was told to read, besides the bible, was a book called "Spirit Controlled Temperament" by Tim Lahaye. This book enlightened my understanding about temperaments. I now realized how important it is for families to understand the way they were created by God as unique individuals. Each family member is given a specific temperament out of which their personality arises. This temperament is unique to the individual and we are to help them develop in the way that God intended. I discovered I was trying to conform others to the way God had made me. This book was simple and exactly what I needed at that time.

***

"Temperament is the combination of inborn traits that subconsciously affects all of our behavior." These traits, which are passed on by our genes, are based on hereditary factors and arranged at the time of conception. (see reference on Copyright page.)

***

There are many theories related to temperaments and how they relate to the human body and personality. One of the first people to develop a theory regarding how medicine and temperament are related was Hippocrates around 400 B.C.

Hippocrates a Greek physician and philosopher incorporated the four "humors"/temperaments into his medical theories. This theory was a part of the ancient medical concept of Humorism, which suggested a correlation between bodily fluids and human personality traits and behaviors. Although his theory of excess bodily fluids as the origin of temperament was disproven, the concept of four basic personality types has formed the basis of many other behavioral theories.

At the time we read Tim LaHaye´s simple book on the four basic temperaments and how to let the Holy Spirit control your specific temperament, it was very helpful in enabling us to identify some major problems that we (mostly I) had in our relationship. There are several teachings on temperaments today and I do not recommend anyone seek out great intellectual understanding about temperaments. Personally, I am the kind of person who gets confused if you make something too complicated and it seems to lose the life and the reality it is supposed to give.

I teach and encourage individuals to understand how they were made by God and to love not only the way that God made you, but also the way that God made others. Therefore, I will now give some instruction about what I believe are the four basic temperaments. I feel most people will be strong in one or two of the temperaments. Two of the basic temperaments are focused on being outward and two of the temperaments are focused on living more on the inside.

Extroverted Temperament: The *Choleric* and *Sanguine* temperaments are more "out-going," more sociable, and more comfortable in a crowd, even standing out in a crowd.

Introverted Temperament: The *Melancholy* and *Phlegmatic* temperaments are more shy and "reserved" and feel anxious about being in a crowd, especially at being singled-out in a crowd.

Now, let's look a little at the four basic temperaments.

Sanguine: People with this temperament tend to be playful, lively, sociable, carefree, talkative, and pleasure-seeking. They may be warm-hearted and optimistic. They make new friends easily, can be imaginative and artistic, and often have many ideas. They can be flighty and changeable; thus sanguine personalities may struggle with following tasks all the way through. The

Sanguine temperament is easy to be around because of their warm and bubbly personality. They will quickly react to some outside stimuli that touches their feelings, whereas a phlegmatic or melancholy or choleric may not show what they are feeling. Feelings are more in control of a sanguine, whereas reflective thinking is more in control of a melancholy or choleric. In a gathering of several individuals, a sanguine's presence will brighten the atmosphere. On the other hand a person may not even be aware when someone with a phlegmatic or melancholy temperament has walked into the room.

Melancholy: People with this temperament may appear serious, introverted, cautious or even suspicious. They can become preoccupied with the tragedy and cruelty in the world and are susceptible to depression and moodiness. They may be focused and conscientious. They often prefer to do things themselves, both to meet their own standards and because they are not inherently sociable. This individual is very gifted and he is not satisfied with doing a good job, with him, it needs to be perfect. He is also very meticulous in his thinking and evaluation of different problems. One of the problems that a melancholy will face is his moodiness. He tends to think deeply about life and situations, but if he does not exercise himself much in the virtue of praise, he lives in the situation at hand, instead of living in the Presence of God. This person can be filled with joy one moment and then full of discouragement the next. Things like the mental disease of introspection can be a tormenting factor in Mr. Melancholy's life. When he is tempted to turn inward on himself, he must make a choice to turn upward and outward and see God and enjoy people. Basically, melancholies will not have an easy time making friends, but when they are your friend, they will be the most faithful. Melancholy people are not prone to take upon themselves a new adventure because they have to feel that they can accomplish a task to the highest degree.

Choleric: People with this temperament tend to be egocentric and extroverted. They may be excitable, impulsive, and restless, with reserves of aggression, energy, and/or passion, and will try to instill that in others. They tend to be task-oriented people and are focused on getting a job done efficiently; their motto is usually "do it now." They can be ambitious, strong-willed and like to be in charge. They can show leadership, are good at planning, and are often practical and solution-oriented. They appreciate receiving respect and esteem for their work. These individuals can make excellent leaders if they learn to be merciful and patient with their followers. Cholerics thrive on activity and find it difficult when they have nothing to do. They must be doing something in order to gain a sense of worth in their life. Adversity and opposition tends to encourage these people to press on to win the war, they are determined people that do not like to lose any battle. I firmly believe that temperaments are received at birth and therefore, a choleric is always leading, even as a two year child with adults. It is inborn to take charge and lead in any given situation. Cholerics will be greatly deprived if they are not allowed to fulfill their God given ability to lead and advance the cause of progress in life.

Phlegmatics: This temperament is usually cool, calm, and very composed; at least if you are looking at him from the outside. People with this temperament may be inward, private, thoughtful, reasonable, calm, patient, caring, and tolerant. They tend to have a rich inner life, seek a quiet peaceful atmosphere, and are content with themselves. They tend to be steadfast, consistent in their habits, and thus steady and faithful friends. This personality type does not like conflict, because it destroys their calm, reticent way of living. The Phlegmatic very much enjoys life when it is sunny and peaceful outside with very little wind blowing. This calm, easy going individual never seems to be affected by what is happening around him. Deep inside of this temperament is a kind, feeling, compassionate person, but seldom will they let others know what they are feeling. This individual has a deep appreciation for the arts, flowers and the beautiful things in life. One weakness in a phlegmatic is their desire to avoid getting too involved in activities and life. This makes it very hard to motivate them to see the possibilities of accomplishing great things and they are very reluctant to adventure into anything unknown. They will do a fantastic job leading once it has been put upon them because of their sense of responsibility and patience.

When I discovered how temperaments work and that each temperament was good and there was no such thing as a bad temperament, my attitude towards Marie greatly changed. Brothers, let us be aware of the danger of our masculine pride, which will try to convince us that the way we are is better than the way our wife is. Pride will convince me that if only my wife could be more like me everything would be better. This is absolutely false and it will cause a husband to try to change his wife, instead of becoming full of compassion. Since opposites attract, a man will often marry a girl that has the opposite temperament of him. This will result in their different temperaments clashing. If they are unaware of the strengths and weaknesses that they each possess; they will start to make judgments on their spouse for his or her behavior. Their hearts will begin to harden and they might start resenting each other. Anything that makes the heart hard will start to destroy the love in a relationship. We must always guard our hearts against cold-love towards the one that God has entrusted to us for life.

Once I learned that my temperament was totally different than Marie's temperament, I realized that Marie was just being the person that she was created to be. She did not have a problem at all. If there was a problem, it was only a lack of understanding of the basic nature of the temperaments.

An understanding of the basic temperaments will also facilitate the godly training of children. Parents can allow their children to learn the way they are formed within instead of trying to make them learn and act as their siblings. God made each person unique with specific qualities and each temperament has specific strengths and weaknesses. The more I understand how we are created, the more I can love myself and others. I conclude this section by agreeing with the Lord when he told Hosea, "For a lack of knowledge, my people are destroyed" (Hosea 4:6a). I believe it is a fair statement to say that our marriage would not be as wonderful as it is if we did not receive the knowledge of human temperaments.

CHAPTER TEN

SELFLESS SEX

A book on marriage that does not talk about sex cannot be a complete book. This subject is so important in order to find fulfillment in a marital relationship. There are many problems relating to sex, but for some reason this is a topic that is seldom discussed. Therefore, the frustrations connected to it many times remain unresolved. I believe the evil one has a specific strategy to cause problems for Christian couples in the area of the bedroom. Some of these problems include: not having sex, not enjoying each other when you do have sex, pornography and sexual sin that replaces real excitement and sexual satisfaction. In other words, if a husband and wife do not enjoy each other physically, the devil will supply a substitute in the form of pornography or masturbation.

Some problems couples experience related to sex include, having hard feelings towards each other in the bedroom, a tremendous lack of honesty, and an attitude of anger or resentment during intercourse. These negative attitudes could cause the couple to focus on another person or another thing during sex. Because love is not filling their hearts towards one another they could enter in to the danger of daydreaming.

Daydreaming or fantasying can be an invisible doorway into the demonic realm. When a person fantasizes about another person's body, this will create a fantasy bond with the other person. There is an invisible world and the only safe way to access that other world is through Jesus Christ. If a person's mind fantasizes or is intoxicated or passive through drug abuse; this will connect them to the dark world of spiritual powers. Satan knows how destructive fantasizing is to the well-being of a person, therefore he will create sex shops and pornographic material that will cause a person to lust after another in their heart. Jesus said that if a man lusts after a woman in his heart; then he has already committed adultery. "But I-I say to you, that everyone who is looking on a woman to desire her, did already commit adultery with her in his heart." (Young's Literal Translation Matthew 5:28).

Within the world, sex is glamorized as a fun, exciting time to enjoy oneself and to be very focused on what makes you feel good. Worldly sex is a very selfish form of sex. There are too many Christian couples that do not enjoy sex or have difficulties in the area of sexual relationship with their spouse. From the beginning of creation it was God's plan for a man and woman to be joined together physically and to multiply and enjoy each other sexually. However, the evil one also had a plan to destroy the joy of sexual union. The evil one desires people of the world to enjoy sexual union, but to make God's children miserable during sex. I often am confronted by a believer's woes due to not being loved by his or her spouse in a physical way. Many times they share with pain how they haven't had sex with their spouse for months or even years. This is very sad and can only leave a person with deep feelings of pain, sorrow, rejection and anger.

A man of God once made the statement that a Christian wife should spend as much time preparing a love feast for her husband as she spends preparing a meal for her family. Christians should not be embarrassed when talking about sex. Sex is a God-given blessing to a man and a woman. Since God created man and woman's bodies to procreate, then sex is a heavenly creation. Embarrassment when discussing sexual issues is a form of disrespect to God's creation.

Whenever marriage is looked at as something negative and unspiritual this can be an open doorway to a religious spirit concerning sexual relations. Paul describes a seducing spirit which brings a doctrine forbidding marriage (1Timothy 4:1, 3). He also says that God *"gives us richly all things to enjoy"* and the *"marriage bed is honorable and the bed is undefiled"* (1Timothy 6:17, Hebrews 13:4). Therefore, whatever God made is good, and every good thing God made has an intended purpose that ultimately reveals His own glory. When a conservative Christian responds to the subject of sex with embarrassment or fear, this slanders the goodness of God and hides His glory. We are called upon to reveal God's goodness and glory in the things that God has given us to enjoy such as sexual union in the bond of marriage.

A Christian is called to deny himself daily (Luke 9:23). This includes in his sexual relationship with his spouse. The world will use sex as a tool to gratify self, but a Christian should use sex as another means of denying self. Selfless sex is to deny yourself so much that you offer your body in love to your spouse. You put her or him above yourself and you give him/her a love gift called your body.

Paul says the body is for the Lord and the Lord is for the body (1 Corinthians 6:13c). The Lord Jesus is always first and then the spouse is second. 1 Corinthians 7:4 says that "the wife does not have power over her own body, but the husband, and likewise also the husband has not power of his own body, but the wife." The body of a Christian husband belongs to his wife and the body of a Christian wife belongs to her husband. This is one reason why a spouse should take care of their body because it is the property of the other. If I do not take care of my body; this is like me borrowing my wife's car and not fixing the tires, changing the oil, or keeping it clean. Instead, she finds that I have left food crumbs on the seat, and trash on the floor of her car. Since my body is not my own, but belongs to my wife; then how I treat my body is how I am taking care of Marie's property.

Heart issues are the key to a fantastic marriage with your spouse. If my heart is clean and full of love, then I will not struggle with sharing my feelings and giving my body and enjoying sex regularly with my spouse. When I speak hard or hold a judgment towards my wife; I will then humble myself and ask her to forgive me. If there are no hidden issues in my heart, then there will be love, truth and joy when I am with my wife. For example, if I have resentment towards my mother because she tried to control me as a child, then I will have a bad attitude towards Marie in our marriage. If there is bitterness toward a brother and I have judgments towards other Christians; then my heart will be easily triggered by things that my wife says and does in my presence.

God created our bodies to have desires for the opposite sex. It was God who said, *"That it is not good for man to be alone"* (Genesis 2:18). For a man to be joined to a woman is God's idea. The thought that it is not good for a man to be without a helpmeet, came from the heart of a perfect Being called God. God created woman to be with a man and He created man with desires to be with the woman. Sex is designed by a Perfect Being, who believes with his perfect understanding, that it will not be good if man does not have a woman by his side. *"He who finds a wife finds a good thing and obtains favor from the Lord."* (Prov. 18:22). God says that when a man finds his wife he has found a good thing and the Lord gives him favor. Men should treat woman as a gift from God. This special gift will increase their blessings and favor from their heavenly father.

One could say that the whole plan of family began with a perfect Creator, who planned two individuals to have a perfect relationship based on His perfect love. If the heart is not being triggered and selfish thoughts are not dominating one's mind; then there can be kind thoughts of each partner. A kind thought about your spouse will result in a kind word and a kind word will produce a kind action. *Kindness is the spiritual secret to having great joy in a selfless sexual relationship with your spouse.*

The husband should focus on loving his wife just as Christ loves his church. This love will be a pure, selfless love that is full of mercy and tenderness towards all people, but especially his wife. A wife should focus on submitting to her husband with a lowly, gentle attitude of respect and love. She should be the support under her husband by encouraging him, especially in times of discouragement. A husband is called to be the leader of his family, but there are usually fears about leading particularly in a spiritual sense. He will fear of inadequacy as a spiritual leader for his wife and children. A wife can greatly encourage him through her kind, thoughtful words. If a wife makes her husband feel totally inferior, he can develop a hopeless attitude about being the leader that God intends for him.

Proverbs 5:18-20 (English Standard Version) *"Let your fountain be blessed, and rejoice in the wife of your youth, a lovely deer, a graceful doe. Let her breasts fill you at all times with delight; be intoxicated always in her love. Why should you be intoxicated; my son, with a forbidden woman and embrace the bosom of an adulteress?"* These scriptures are admonishing a husband to be blessed in his sexual times with his wife. Secondly, it is saying that a husband should rejoice always and be delighted in his wife's breasts. Lastly, these verses are saying a husband should be intoxicated with great pleasure in loving his wife's body. The writer of this proverb closes by saying "why should a husband be intoxicated with the breast another woman?" What a strong, passionate portion of scripture. It could only come from a passionate God that wants his children to live their whole life in his love. Man's calling is to live inside of the very love of God's heart.

As I live my life in the heart of God; then love will start to consume my thoughts, feelings and actions. This love must flow out of me into others because God's pure love can never seek its own (1 Corinthians 13:5). The first one to receive this love flowing out of my heart should be the one closest to me and that would be my wife. Our sexual life should be filled with a passionate love because our God is a passionate Lover. The love of God always comes with passion. According to Proverbs 5:18-20, a husband should always be joyful in his wife's breasts and he should be intoxicated and overflowing with delight in just physically loving her. Otherwise, since it is never good for a man to be alone, he could seek comfort at the breasts or physical features of another woman. I would like to give a real life illustration of how some husbands will be defeated by the evil one.

First, he is full of rejection and hates himself as a person. Secondly, his wife has been in a religious church that does not feel it is right to show emotion or passion to your husband. Sex is treated as something only for the purpose of child-bearing. Now, the wife of this man will not express her desire for her husband and he will not be delighted in their sexual times together. Their hearts will start to become hardened towards each other and their desire for intimacy will decrease. Now, he goes to a McDonald's and right next door is a sex store with a beautiful woman showing her breasts and her countenance is showing every man she desires him. If a man has been rejected by many people, he'll need his wife's acceptance and desire for him. Otherwise, these pornographic type images will appeal to his need of acceptance.

Women are different, they need to be touched. They are affected by touch; whereas men are affected by sight. A woman is emotionally stirred by feeling and her senses being activated by a romance novel or by someone touching her body. A man is emotionally, physically stimulated by what he sees. Therefore, a romance novel can have almost the same effect on a woman as pornography can have on a man. A husband should speak kind words to his wife and touch her gently and affectionately.

Let us pursue this to make it even more practical. Here are some points to consider:

How a husband appears outwardly to his wife as well as the way he touches her is very important. The way a husband's breath and body smell is a practical issue that he must give attention to. He needs to make his wife feel that he desires her to be close to him. Therefore, quick and sweet hugs and kisses are always appropriate for husbands to give their wives. This is actually a form of showing honor to the God-given gift of sex within a marriage.

A wife should show her husband that she really desires him to touch her and that she desires his physical companionship in bed. If a wife never dresses in a provocative way for her husband in bed; this could be sending a message to him that she does not really desire him. If a husband does not feel that his wife desires him and then he sees other women dressing very provocative and showing him that they desire him, this could be a demonic set up to entice him. Satan will try to entrap the husband into a fantasy bond or a real sexual bond with another person. This will form an ungodly soul tie with the husband and another person. All ungodly soul-ties formed through fantasy bonds or sexual encounters must be severed by the Lord Jesus Christ. After the ungodly soul-ties have been broken, then a godly soul tie can be formed between a husband and wife.

Since God is passionate, full of zeal and pure love; it is the goal of religious spirits to create a hard cold love within a marriage. Religious Spirits will cause Christian couples to perform the outward sexual act in a formal and cold way.

Religious spirits thrive on a cold form of sexual love between couples. This must be rejected and true passionate love from God should fill the hearts of the couple. The words spirituality and sex no longer have to be separate entities. A religious spirit will fill the heart of a person so that they will not have true joy in physically embracing their spouse. Sex is holy and created by God for his people to enjoy each other in a loving physical way. Out of an intense, loving and passionate experience will come godly fruit. The fruit of a passionate love encounter will manifest as emotionally healthy offspring and experiencing blessed times as a family.

The offspring of this godly couple will be full of life, joy, health and vitality. If a couple has sex in the midst of intense love, the fruit of the woman's womb will be abounding with blessings and no fear. Perfect love casts out fear. If a baby is conceived in anger, then the little embryo could be covered in a canopy of fear and oppression. If a couple is passionate and delightfully embracing, kissing and loving each other the fruit of this relationship will be covered in love and safety.

My dear brothers and sisters, let us consider these scriptures concerning sex. Proverbs 5:18-20 says "a husband should be enthralled, delighted and joyful with his wife's body". Hebrews 13:4 says "the marriage bed is undefiled." Genesis 2:18 says "it is not good for a man to be alone" 1 Corinthians 7:4 says, "the wife does not have the right over her body but the husband, and the husband does not have power over his body, but he wife does."

With so many truths that emphasize the goodness and holiness of sex; what comes to your mind when you hear the word sex? Is marital sex good? If the answer is yes, then great marital sex would be even better. Is marital sex holy? If yes, then great marital sex would also be holy. Is marital sex a demonstration of love? If yes, then great marital sex is a demonstration of love. We must be freed from the cloud of defilement that seems to surround the topic of sex; even Christian godly sex.

Christian godly marital sex is selfless. Selfless sex is when a partner denies himself and puts his spouse first. His desire is to please her. He desires her to have the first orgasm. He desires that she would feel special about herself and therefore, he would not speak negatively about her appearance. He would encourage her in any possible way; such as speech, touch, and honor. He would bless his wife at night while they hold each other in bed. He would never force his wife to do anything she would not want to do. He would be very sensitive to the needs of his wife. Lastly, he would make his wife feel she is desirable, and that he desires to be with her. Selfless sex for a wife would include all of the same things that are listed above. She would do all of the same things to her husband as he would do to her. This is the secret to having the greatest joy in sex. Both partners totally deny themselves, putting the other first. Since both are giving all; now both are also receiving all and their joy is complete.

I want to make one final remark concerning the importance of sex in a marriage. Many studies have shown the advantages and the benefits of sexual intercourse. Some of the benefits of experiencing a healthy, normal sex life are:

1. Stress is released
2. The physical body stays healthier
3. Sleep is better
4. Hormones which are released that cause a person to feel good about themselves.
5. Emotional issues are alleviated due to the innate pleasure of feeling good about oneself.

CHAPTER ELEVEN

A CHECKLIST FOR FOLLOWERS OF THE FLAME

Once a marriage has been totally healed and transformed by God, it is important for each partner to maintain the flame of a fantastic marriage. There are several points that should be reviewed on a daily basis to make sure that a person is still pursuing a fantastic marriage. If I notice the flame has diminished, I should check over this list, and it is quite possible that the main reason will be discovered.

1. **Am I walking in the narrow way?** "Therefore all things whatsoever ye would that men should do to you, do ye even so to them: for this is the law and the prophets… Because strait is the gate, and narrow is the way, which leadeth unto life, and few there be that find it" (Matthew 7:12, 14).

The narrow way is when a person desires to be treated in some way (kindness, soft words, thoughtfulness, blessing, etc.), he should first relate to his spouse in the very way he is wanting his spouse to relate to him. Am I treating my spouse the very way that I want her to treat me? Examples: Do I want him to touch me? Am I touching him? I want him to be more affectionate with me. Am I being affectionate with him? Are we treating others exactly the way we desire them to treat us?

2. **Am I seeking the kingdom of God and his righteousness in my life?** "Seek ye first the kingdom of God and His righteousness and all these things shall be added unto you" (Matthew 6:33).

Jesus states that if I will put his kingdom and his righteousness first in my life, all these other things will be added unto me and this includes a fantastic marriage. A marriage or a tremendous family must not be first in my life. God's kingdom and God's righteousness must be first. In order for me to be a kingdom seeker, I must put God's interests above mine. The apostle Paul said that all men were seeking their own interests and not the interests of Jesus Christ.

A kingdom seeker is always looking out for the things that will advance the kingdom of God in his city: This becomes more and more natural as a person practices being kingdom minded first at home and then outside the home. Part of being kingdom minded is to see yourself connected to an entire body of believers within your specific city. You do not see just your own family or your own church, group, or culture, but you see the entire body of Christ of which you are a major part within an area.

3. **Am I taking the blame for bad attitudes and harsh words to my spouse and children?** God says, "If we confess our sins, he is faithful and just to forgive us our sins, and to cleanse us from all unrighteousness" (1 John 1:9).

Have I been taking the blame for my sins or have I just been concentrating on the sins of my spouse? When was the last time I asked forgiveness from someone in my family?

If I truly desire my children and spouse to humble themselves and to ask forgiveness of each other, then I should set the example, especially if I am the spiritual head of the home. *"Confess your faults one to another and pray for one another that ye may be healed"* (James 5:16a).

Jesus took the blame for the sins of the entire world. We have seen many times when a mother or father will humble themselves, how their humbling affects their own children. It is always positive, and God will do softening in the hearts of their children.

4. **Is the law of kindness on my lips?** See Proverbs 31:26. Do I think kind thoughts? Do I speak kind words? Kind thoughts lead to kind words, and kind words lead to kind actions. Kindness has a tremendous power to change the atmosphere of the home. When kindness is not present in the parents, often the atmosphere in their home is tense and lacks peace.

5. **Am I a broken vessel for Father God to pour his gentleness through me?** Out of the heart of kindness will flow divine gentleness. David said that it was God's gentleness that made him great. See Psalm 18:35b. The one major reason that David was such a great man was that he experienced the very gentleness of God. The best time to show godly gentleness to my spouse or children is when they have failed.

6. **Am I letting the mind of Christ be in me today?** Let this mind be in you, which was also in Christ Jesus. See Philippians 2:5.

This mind of Christ refers to five basic attitudes of the heart.

- Not esteeming what you deserve. (I do not claim what is rightfully mine to claim.)
- Esteeming others as better than yourself.
- Taking the form of a servant.
- Humbling yourself (when my heart wants to be lifted up, I must bring it down.)
- Making yourself of no reputation (Not being concerned about how others are viewing you). Only concerning yourself about how God is beholding you. Is the same attitude of the heart that was in Christ Jesus living inside of my heart today toward myself, my spouse, and my children?

7. **Are there any hard, stony feelings inside of my heart towards anybody?** Is my heart sweet and tender or is it hard on the inside?

8. **Am I asking Jesus to look through my eyes at my spouse and to feel through my heart at my spouse and children, or am I depending on myself to live the Christian life?**

9. **Am I totally committed to a lifestyle of love?** Proverbs 28:9 says, *"He that turneth away his ear from hearing the law, even his prayer shall be abomination."* When I turn my ear away from hearing the law (the fulfillment of the law is love), then my prayers become an abomination in God's sight. Am I committed to walking in love in my thoughts toward my fellowman?

10. **Am I cherishing a thankful heart?** The Lord commands us to give thanks always. My attitude should be thank-

ful, rejoicing, and an attitude of need and trust, which is a prayerful spirit. Rejoice evermore, pray without ceasing, and in everything give thanks: for this is the will of God in Christ Jesus concerning you, quench not the Spirit. Have I put out the fire of the Holy Spirit by a refusal to give thanks and praise God? This grieves the Holy Spirit and puts out the fire of his love. The most necessary fire is to praise God during times when things do not appear to be going good. Praise must declare Jesus is victor at these times. When I have an attitude of praise and thanksgiving, this will create an atmosphere of peace and joy within my home, and it will have more power than the power of negative thoughts or words from others within my family or home. The power of the love of God is greater than the power of the evil one to create a negative atmosphere. Good will overcome evil.

11. **Am I living my life in faith?** Without faith, we cannot please God. Anything that is not of faith is sin. By faith, we are to believe and expect Jesus Christ to live inside of our body. He will live his own perfect life by his Holy Spirit inside of my heart, and he will write his laws on my heart and put them in my mind. Faith must receive the power and blessings of God's presence to saturate my heart and life on a daily basis. Without him and his presence, we can do nothing.

If we are really committed to having a fantastic marriage, then taking the time to go over this checklist until it becomes our very nature will not be seen as a burden but as a delight.

May the Lord enable us by his grace to go over this checklist and by his Holy Spirit to be committed to each point.

EPILOGUE

Dear brothers and sisters, in this book I have tried by the Holy Spirit to describe in a practical way how to enter into the victory that was accomplished at the cross of the Lord Jesus Christ. The Word of God says that he is constantly giving us his victory through Jesus Christ every moment of every day. See 1 Corinthians 15:58, 2 Corinthians 2:14. The only way that we can experience what Jesus has done for us is for us to take all the evil that affects us personally to the cross and allow the mercy of God to disintegrate the power of the evil. His mercy triumphs over judgment. We can demand judgment against a person that has sinned against us, but then we must also demand judgment and justice for every single evil thing that we have also committed. Whatever we want others to receive, we likewise will receive. Calvary demands that all men could receive mercy if they will ask for it and give it to others. To live a lifestyle of mercy and true compassion is to demonstrate the power of the cross in the beauty of holiness. The cross has conquered all evils, and when we take up our cross, we are living in victory.

Throughout this book, it has been emphasized that the secret to a fantastic marriage is learning how to experience and release the real presence of Jesus Christ into the inner man of husband and wife. It has also been emphasized that there is another presence that is also real in our world. This evil presence causes much pain and hurt, and it is set upon destroying every marriage. It can be correctly stated that as a couple removes the presence of evil from their hearts and receives the presence of God into their hearts, the very love of God will saturate their individual lives, their marriage, and their family. Their home will be a haven of rest, and their marriage will be well on its way to becoming a fantastic marriage. This is not only possible, but it is also very practical.

May the eyes of all who read this book be enlightened to see the hope that God has for every marriage through the grace and love of his Son, our Lord Jesus Christ.

In summary, the purpose for marriage is to demonstrate how much God loves his bride. God is love and he refers to his people as his bride, and he draws them with cords of love. The husband is to show the world how much God loves. When the world sees how much a husband loves his wife, they will understand how much Jesus loves his church. When a wife loves her husband in lowly submission, she is demonstrating how much the church loves Christ through its submission.

Throughout this book the husband and wife relationship was explored to see what things hinder it and what things cause it to flourish. Some things that hinder a fantastic marriage are:

- Pride (chapter two)
- Husbands that uncover their wives (chapter three)
- Unbelief, disappointments, a broken heart, demonic strongholds, judgments, inner vows and self effort (chapter four)
- Dishonoring one another (chapter five)
- Passivity and anger (chapter six)

Some things that create a fantastic marriage are:

- Humility (chapter two)
- Husbands that cover their wives (chapter three)
- Giving honor to each other (chapter five)
- Husbands which fulfill their role as a priest and king (chapter six)
- Wives who see their value and importance to bless their husbands (chapter seven)
- The manifest presence of God within the home (chapter eight).

All of life is evolving around many choices that each person makes every single day. In order for a couple to truly have a fantastic marriage they must choose to pursue it with all of their heart. At the very center of a fantastic marriage will be an unquenchable flame. This unquenchable fire is the very heart of God, "for our God is a consuming fire." See Hebrews 12:29. One of his names is everlasting burnings. In the Song of Songs, it is stated that "many waters cannot quench love and the floods cannot drown it." Nothing has enough power to quench the fire of a heart filled with love. This is the heart that Jesus describes in the greatest sermon ever preached, called the Sermon on the Mount. Jesus in his sermon describes a heart that is pure, merciful and extremely blessed. This heart is the Master's very own heart. Both the love of a groom and the submission of a bride is found in the heart of Jesus. The heart described by Jesus loves his enemies. Jesus even went so far as to die for his enemies and through Jesus we also can love our enemies.

All of these attitudes of the heart should be lived out through Jesus Christ in the relationship between a believer and his enemy.

Now, if we are to live this way toward our enemy, then how much more are we to live this way before our spouse? If I am to love my enemy when he says all kinds of evil falsely against me, then I should surely love my husband when he says evil and negative things about me. If I am to do to others what I want them to do to me, then surely I should do to my wife what I desire that she would do to me. If I should pray for that one that despitefully uses me, then surely I should pray for my wife if she rejects me and accuses me. If I am to think more highly of others then I do of myself, then surely I should think more highly of my spouse than I do of myself. One final comment: in order to find a fantastic marriage, I should be totally committed to living my Christianity, first and foremost, in my home with my family. This should have the highest priority in a believer. Our Christian life must first be demonstrated with those who are closest to us, and then it can be demonstrated to our neighbors, church, friends, then our enemies, and then to the farthest ends of the earth. A fantastic marriage will be experienced by a person who is totally committed to living in the very life of Jesus. The same life that rose from the dead is now living in each member of his spiritual body on earth. It is this very life that makes a marriage fantastic. When a marriage is fantastic, then Christianity will be fantastic. When Christianity is fantastic, then the world will believe in a fantastic God. This is the God who sent his only Son into the world so that the world could live their lives through him. He desires for couples to experience a wonderful marriage by his grace. May the Lord richly enable you to experience a fantastic marriage to the furthering of His glorious kingdom.

A CLOSING PRAYER

Father, I thank you for your plan and for my family. Thank you that you desire to fill my life with peace, joy and love. Thank you that Jesus died so that we could live. Forgive me for all hard feelings inside of my heart and wash me clean. Jesus, take over my life and love through me. I forgive everyone that has hurt me and I choose today to love others as you have loved me. Amen.

Sharing the heart of the Lamb,
Greg Violi

OTHER BOOKS BY GREG VIOLI

Depression and Introspection: Healing for the Diseased Mind:
This book explains root causes for depression and how the disease of introspection affects millions. Greg discusses how it blocks a person from living in the presence of God and how a person can walk in freedom.

The Lamb's Heart
This book is a thorough revelation of the spiritual heart and the heart of God. It has much truth concerning brokenness in the Father's heart and how to allow the Father to heal your own brokenness. There is a tremendous revelation concerning how and why God always looks at the heart.

The King's Holy Beauty
This book is the revelation of the secret mystery hidden in the heart of Father God. It is a revelation given by the Holy Spirit to unveil the Beauty of Holiness. Since the book has been distributed there have been many testimonies of the changed lives of the people who have read it.

Whose Image and Which Mind
This book discusses the differences between heavenly and earthly wisdom, the heavenly image and the earthly demonic image. Through this book you can discover the splendor of living life through the heart of the Lamb and being fed from the river of divine wisdom!

Called to be Kings and Priests
In this book the purpose of a Godly Father and Husband are revealed through the scriptures. It is also revealed how to live out God's purposes of a man practically and how to heal wounds created by men not fulfilling God's calling on men.

A Heavenly Victorious Life

The Spirit of the ascended Christ desires to come inside of a believer and reveal Himself. When we allow Him to do this it produces a heavenly life, one always abounding in victory. Greg describes the real life of the ascended, exalted Lord and how we can abide in the fullness that He offers.

The Key to Staying in Love

God desires mercy more than any sacrifice that man can offer. In any relationship, the most desirable attributes are kindness, mercy and love. When a person allows outward appearances or possessions to take first priority, judgements and hardness become the replacement for a heart attitude of kindness. The love of God cannot abide where there is hardness of heart. In this small booklet, you can learn how judgements operate and how to guard yourself from destructive attitudes.

For more information about Greg Violi, his ministry,
and his itinerary visit the following website:
www.greg-violi.com/en

To contact or invite Greg Violi please email:
greg.violi.ministries@gmail.com

For sermons from Greg Violi visit our YouTube channel:
Greg Violi Ministries

52709731R00066

Made in the USA
Charleston, SC
24 February 2016